T0213826

SpringerBriefs in Service Science

SpringerBriefs present concise summaries of cutting-edge research and practical applications across a wide spectrum of fields. Featuring compact volumes of 50 to 125 pages, the series covers a range of content from professional to academic.

Typical publications can be:

A timely report of state-of-the art methods

A bridge between new research results, as published in journal articles

A snapshot of a hot or emerging topic

An in-depth case study

A presentation of core concepts that students must understand in order to make independent contributions

SpringerBriefs are characterized by fast, global electronic dissemination, standard publishing contracts, standardized manuscript preparation and formatting guidelines, and expedited production schedules.

The rapidly growing fields of Big Data, AI and Machine Learning, together with emerging analytic theories and technologies, have allowed us to gain comprehensive insights into both social and transactional interactions in service value co-creation processes. The series SpringerBriefs in Service Science is devoted to publications that offer new perspectives on service research by showcasing service transformations across various sectors of the digital economy. The research findings presented will help service organizations address their service challenges in tomorrow's service-oriented economy.

Qiang Su

Healthcare Operations Management

A Holistic Care Chain Perspective

Qiang Su
School of Economics and Management
Tongji University
Shanghai, China

ISSN 2731-3743 ISSN 2731-3751 (electronic)
SpringerBriefs in Service Science
ISBN 978-3-031-13396-1 ISBN 978-3-031-13397-8 (eBook)
https://doi.org/10.1007/978-3-031-13397-8

This Springer imprint is published by the registered company Springer Nature Switzerland AG
The registered company address is: Gewerbestrasse 11, 6330 Cham, Switzerland

Acknowledgement

This work is supported by the National Natural Science Foundation of China (NSFC) (Grant Nos. 71972146 and 71974127).

Contents

Chapter 1
Introduction to the Healthcare Operations Management

Medical services directly impact people's safety and quality of life. Compared with other services, medical services are particularly complex. This complexity is derived from three facets: First, there is the complexity of illness itself, including the complexity of the human body and pathogenesis; second, there is the complexity of the diagnosis and treatment process, including diagnostic techniques and treatment protocols; and third, there are complexities such as doctor–patient behaviours, medical ethics, and socioeconomic factors. To ensure high-quality service in a complex environment, improving the management of medical services is increasingly important.

The management of medical services refers to the planning, organisation, guidance, and supervision activities performed in the process of rendering medical services. The goal of this is to implement the effective operation of all departments of a medical organisation and to guarantee the quality and safety of its medical services. Along with the expansion of medical reform and opening of the healthcare market, the traditional hospital management model has failed to adapt to the needs of new circumstances. Innovation in medical services and improvements made to hospital management are eagerly expected by patients and medical practitioners. In this situation, some advanced management approaches such as operation optimisation, industrial engineering, lean production, and Six Sigma can be employed to support healthcare operations improvement [1]. The author and his team members have been conducting nearly 20 years of exploration in healthcare operations enhancement. The materials of this book are almost all derived from the author and his team's research achievements and the real case study results of improvements to the management of medical services. Hopefully, this book will provide readers with some thoughts and enlightenment.

Q. Su, *Healthcare Operations Management*, SpringerBriefs in Service Science,
https://doi.org/10.1007/978-3-031-13397-8_1

1.1   Trends in the Development of Medical Management

Medical management has paid increasing attention to the application of information technology and data analysis techniques [2–4]. Lang stated in *Science* that the development of electronic technologies, especially the development of mobile networks and data sharing, will significantly advance global medical research [5]. Powell emphasised, also in *Science*, the importance of disease prevention and pointed out that disease prevention depends to a large extent on the integration of data from different electronic health information systems [6].

Via an extensive review of the literature, we have summarised the four latest trends in the development of medical management research:

1. The transformation from in-hospital diagnosis and treatment to diagnosis-and-treatment chain. The stages of disease prevention, onset, diagnosis, treatment, and rehabilitation are supported by different medical efforts distributed across time and space. In other words, diagnosis and treatment activities in different stages, such as early prevention, pre-hospital emergency care, hospitalisation, and rehabilitation therapy, occur in different medical institutions and departments and require the support and coordination of different medical staff, institutions, and equipment. The whole process constitutes a diagnosis-and-treatment chain that spans the whole cycle of health management. Future research needs to break through the traditional thinking that focuses solely on the local optimisation of clinical diagnosis and treatment in a single hospital or a single department, by achieving the whole process optimisation and an optimal allocation of resources along the whole diagnosis-and-treatment chain.
2. The transformation from 'disease medicine' to 'health medicine'. In addition to paying attention to patients already suffering from diseases, future medical diagnosis and treatment will attach greater importance to monitoring, preserving, and intervening in the health of ordinary people to emphasise health management throughout life, starting with disease prevention. Many preventive medicine studies have made clear that for every yuan that is spent on prevention, 8.59 yuan in drug costs can be saved, and approximately 100 yuan are saved on the costs of treatment, missed work, and care-giving.
3. The transformation from personal experience to big data analysis. Big data analysis provides a technical foundation for integrating medical information from all parties and optimising decision-making, which allows medical diagnosis and treatment decisions to stop relying solely on the accumulation of traditional personal medical experience. With the support of multidisciplinary scientific data and evidence, more effective medical decisions and interventions are achieved, and the limited experience of individual doctors is coalesced into a constantly expanding, updating, and self-learning knowledge base that then provides customised disease prevention, emergency treatment, diagnosis and treatment, and rehabilitation management programmes.
4. Placing importance on the self-adaptive and self-learning capabilities of medical service systems. Learning-oriented medical groups monitor the effectiveness of

medical service workflow, resource management, and quality and safety systems via information collection, processing, and analysis to enable constant self-renewal and self-learning based on cumulative medical cases. Meanwhile, information and knowledge sharing in hospitals, communities, and even larger regions can be realised to promote the continuous improvement of medical service systems.

It is not difficult to see that the above four development trends are fully consistent with the basic principles of total quality management (TQM). Among them, trend 1 (the transformation from in-hospital diagnosis and treatment to diagnosis-and-treatment chain) corresponds to the process management principle in TQM, that is, placing importance on the process design, monitoring, and optimisation and improvement of the whole health management cycle. Trend 2 (the transformation from 'disease medicine' to 'health medicine') corresponds to the preventive principle of TQM, that is, emphasising the importance of disease prevention and early treatment. Trend 3 (the transformation from personal experience to big data analysis) corresponds to the measurability principle in TQM, that is, if there are no measurements then there is no way to objectively measure service quality, let alone monitor and improve quality. Furthermore, big data analysis techniques can deepen our understanding of systems and processes, help us to achieve more optimal decision-making, and thus improve the service quality of healthcare. Trend 4 (placing importance on the self-adaptive and self-learning capabilities of medical service systems) corresponds to the continuous improvement of quality management, that is, emphasising the openness, self-feedback, and self-correction capabilities of the system to guarantee the continuous improvement of the system from the perspective of its underlying mechanisms.

The four aforementioned trends in the development of the healthcare service sector have provided direction to research on medical service management, and they can also play a guiding role for the reform of medical and health services in China. Medical service management in China has many shortcomings, such as an emphasis on diagnosis and treatment of disease over disease prevention, emphasis on treatment technology over process management, and emphasis on clinical experience over data analysis. This traditional medical service management model has failed to fulfil the needs of modern society. As a result, there is an urgent need to apply advanced management concepts to carry out innovation and reform in medical service.

1.2   From Clinical Pathways to Diagnosis and Treatment Chains

The service process analysis is the foundation of service management evaluation and improvement. In terms of medical service, research on the diagnosis and treatment process has a long history, and it has gone through two stages one after the other: clinical pathways and then diagnosis-and-treatment chains.

Clinical pathways refer to treatment plans formulated for a specific disease or operation and that have the goal of improving the quality of medical services [7, 8]. Since the 1980s, the clinical pathway management model has been used extensively [9–13]. The implementation of clinical pathways can bring a great deal of benefits to patients and medical institutions. In addition to shortening hospitalisation times and reducing treatment costs, clinical pathways have also been conducive to improving treatment outcomes, reducing complications, increasing patient satisfaction, increasing the participation of patients or nursing staff in the treatment process, and improving communication between doctors and nurses [14–22].

The optimal design of clinical pathways is vital to the improvement of the quality of medical service and process efficiency. However, clinical pathways mainly manage the diagnosis and treatment processes of patients within hospitals and do not pay attention to health management or emergency medical services before admission to hospital, nor do they pay attention to rehabilitation treatment after hospitalisation. Thus, the authors hold that paying attention solely to clinical diagnosis and treatment, this type of local optimisation, is insufficient. In this context, researchers have proposed the concept of diagnosis-and-treatment chains, which has received extensive interest from medical practitioners and researchers [23]. Diagnosis-and-treatment chains consider the entire process of medical services from the perspective of the patients' whole life cycle, including diagnosis and treatment activities in different stages such as health management, pre-hospital emergency care, in-hospital diagnosis and treatment, and rehabilitation therapy. Diagnosis-and-treatment chains can integrate all these activities together into a unified system for synthetical management and optimisation. In China, several hospitals have begun to put the concept of diagnosis-and-treatment chains into practice. Ningxia Medical University studied the effectiveness of the nursing care chain for hip fractures in the elderly in China [24]. The Nanjing General Hospital has established diagnosis-and-treatment chains for more than 10 diseases, such as lung cancer, coronary heart disease, lymphoma, and hepatic cirrhosis [25]. These practical applications have all achieved good social and economic benefits.

However, in the relevant design theory of diagnosis-and-treatment chains, the research is still in its infancy. Existing practical applications are all based on the subjective experience of designers and experts under the guidance of process reengineering theory. With the in-depth development of evidence-based medicine, more scientific and more effective theoretical methods of diagnosis-and-treatment chains are needed to guide practical applications and to better exploit the potential of diagnosis-and-treatment chain optimisation in improving the quality of medical services. Thus, a systematic process design and optimisation approach for diagnosis-and-treatment chains will become an important direction of medical service management research.

1.3 The Blueprint and the Moment of Truth in Medical Services

The diagnosis-and-treatment chain covers a patient's whole life cycle. Specifically, it can be divided into different stages, including health management, pre-hospital emergency care, in-hospital diagnosis and treatment, and rehabilitation therapy. Furthermore, these stages can be divided into three main service processes: pre-hospital services, in-hospital services, and post-hospital services. Among them, pre-hospital services refer primarily to health management and pre-hospital emergency care. In-hospital services refer primarily to medical services that the patients received in hospital, including outpatient and emergency services and inpatient and surgical services. They mainly include disease diagnosis, surgical treatment, and so forth. Post-hospital services refer primarily to rehabilitation therapy activities, which are carried out in community medical institutions or at the patient's home.

According to Qiu's research, the contact points (the moment of truth, MOT) in hospital service are vital to patient satisfaction and the quality assurance of medical services [26]. Svensson believes that we should study the MOTs in depth, particularly from the perspective of service whole life cycle, and that we should explore in depth such problems as service design, service development, service delivery, and service management in stages [27]. Qiu points out that we should rethink the services' contact points and puts forward the concepts of the service contact chain and the service contact network. Qiu also believes that the rapid development of digital and network technology to date has provided the possibility of doing research on service contact chains and service contact networks. To examine service contact chains thoroughly and comprehensively, Qiu proposed that we should focus on the four flows in the service contact chain: (1) Customer experience flow: applying behavioural science and cognitive science to create a better customer experience and to fulfil customers' utilitarian and psychological needs. (2) Organisational behaviour flow: improving employees' job satisfaction by considering the dynamic characteristics of individuals and organisations, organisational behaviour, operations management, and personnel optimisation. (3) Physical flow: ensuring customer experience and employee satisfaction by paying attention to the service delivery process and applying appropriate service tools, scenarios, resources, and so forth. (4) Information flow: supporting operations management decision-making by capturing important data and information in real time via artificial intelligence throughout the whole service life cycle [26].

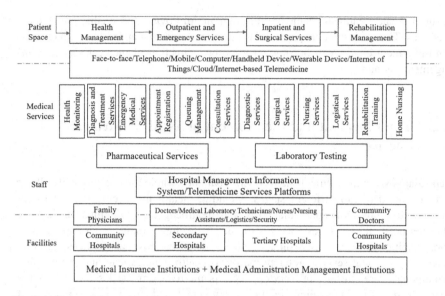

Fig. 1.1 The medical service blueprint for the whole life cycle of patient

Based on the analysis above, the author has designed and proposed a medical service blueprint for the whole life cycle of the patient to identify the service contact points, depict the contact chain (contact network) of medical services, and identify the customer experience flow, organisational behaviour flow, physical flow, and information flow. This figure can serve as a reference framework for medical managers in the evaluation and improvement of medical services.

Figure 1.1 depicts the blueprint for medical services that includes the whole of a patient's diagnosis-and-treatment chain from the health management of the patient/ resident to pre-hospital emergency care, outpatient and emergency services, inpatient and surgical treatment, and rehabilitation therapy. Among them, health management refers to the service rendered via health monitoring and the diagnosis and treatment of common ailments carried out by community hospitals. These are rendered by family physicians or community health workers. Outpatient and emergency services include pre-hospital emergency care and outpatient emergency care. Pre-hospital emergency care is provided by ambulance systems which is named as emergency medical service (EMS). The outpatient and emergency services are provided by secondary and tertiary hospitals, including appointment registration, queuing management, consultation services, pharmaceutical services, and laboratory testing. Inpatient and surgical services take place at secondary or tertiary hospitals and include diagnostic, surgical, nursing, and logistical services. They also require the support of pharmaceutical services and laboratory testing. Rehabilitation management is mostly implemented in community hospitals or patients' homes and includes services such as home caring and rehabilitation training.

All these medical services require the support of network information technology, which includes mobile phones, internet hospitals, wearable devices, and cloud platform. Medical insurance institutions provide medical expense supervision and compensation payment functions. Medical administration institutions are responsible for the supervision and guidance of medical institutions.

The diagnosis-and-treatment chains make up a complex service process. The interdependence of the contact points for medical services at different stages forms a contact chain (contact network) of patient diagnosis and treatment services that include the four flows of medical services. First is the patient experience flow in the patient space (see Fig. 1.1), from health management, pre-hospital emergency care, outpatient and emergency services, and inpatient and surgical services to rehabilitation management. Second is the organisational behaviour flow in the service provider space, which includes medical institutions and their medical care workers at all levels and includes medical insurance institutions and medical administration management departments. Third is the physical flow in the service scenario space, which includes all manner of service facilities and equipment, sites and spaces, computer network systems, and so forth. The last is information flow, which is a medical service system composed of telephones, mobile phones, computers, handheld devices, the internet of things, cloud platforms, and internet telemedicine.

Such a complex system will face many management issues and service bottlenecks in the process of operations management. How to improve the service process and optimise service management has become an urgent problem that needs to be studied. The following summarises some representative operations management issues based on the author's years of research experience.

1.4 The Operations Management Issues in Medical Services

Research on medical service operations management can be traced back to the beginning of the last century, when Frank Bunker Gilbreth applied motion research techniques to the analysis and optimisation of surgical processes in 1913 [28]. In the twenty-first century, along with the rapid development of the service industry, operations management has been applied increasingly in the field of medical services and plays an immense role in fields such as medical service process improvement, resource allocation optimisation, information technology applications, and quality management.

1.4.1 The Improvement of Medical Service Processes

Hospital processes are key to safeguarding medical services. Approximately 110,000 patients die in the United States each year due to improper hospital process design and operational errors. The Institute for Healthcare Improvement (IHI) mentioned in its white paper 'Optimising Patient Flow-Moving Patients Smoothly

Through Acute Care Settings' that, since last-minute postponements and cancellations are extremely common in hospitals, patients and medical staff believe this to be an inevitable part of the medical process. However, the IHI has found by studying more than 50 hospitals that this phenomenon can be eliminated via process optimisation. According to research by IHI, the interaction process between the emergency department, intensive care unit (ICU), operating room, and related departments upstream and downstream from them is the main reason causing delays in service.

In medical institutions, there are many service processes, such as consultation, examination, hospital admission, and physician order execution. These processes are in a constant state of flux, the primary reasons are as follows: (1) The introduction of modern information technology has transformed workflows that were traditionally centred around paper materials. For example, the paper-based medical record management process was changed to electronic medical record management. (2) Changes in relevant policies and regulations can also induce changes in medical processes. (3) The market pursuing for higher level of medical efficiency and quality requires the continuous improvement of medical processes. (4) Advancements in medical technology and the expansion of medical services also require adaptive adjustments to be made to medical service processes.

To support the medical service process improvement, the process analysis technology in operations management is widely used. Generally, process management can be divided into two categories, process improvement and process reengineering. Process improvement emphasises gradual reform while process reengineering emphasises fundamental reform. The following principles need to be followed in the medical service process improving: (1) Processes are the foundation for the assurance of medical services. The organisational framework and departmentalisation of medical institutions must comply with the needs of the medical service processes. (2) The objective of process improvement is patient centric and to improve their satisfaction. (3) Medical process management emphasises process simplification and efficiency improvement. (4) Process management emphasises the coordination and cooperation among medical institutions' departments to jointly pursue the efficiency of processes. (5) Medical service process management emphasises the application of information technology.

In the field of medical service process improvement, a significant amount of research and practical work has been carried out at home and abroad. Sweden's Stockholm Hospital applied process reengineering techniques to redesign surgical procedures. By establishing surgical preparation rooms and carrying out pre-anaesthesia in a timely manner, the waiting time for operations has been reduced successfully. In a bid to reduce congestion and waiting times for emergency patients, Massachusetts General Hospital changed its central laboratory testing model and set up satellite laboratories for point-of-care testing (POCT) in their emergency departments. The average turnover time of patients decreased by 87%, emergency patient waiting time decreased by an average of 41.3 minutes, and patient satisfaction increased significantly [29]. The United Kingdom's Hillingdon Hospital moved its blood testing from a central laboratory to the clinical department where the patient is located, which decreased the waiting time for blood test results from an average of

1 day to just 5 minutes. Australia's Flinders Hospital used lean thinking to implement hospital-wide process reengineering. India's Aravind Hospital is one of the largest eye hospitals in the world. This hospital reorganised and optimised its outpatient system to provide one-stop humanised service and improved the efficiency of medical services and patient satisfaction. In China, scholars have analysed the present situation of emergency procedures in PLA No. 304 Hospital and found the key issues, control points, and the primary reasons affecting the quality of emergency medical treatment. Other scholars analysed the hospitalisation process for common surgeries in general surgery departments and found that by reorganising the hospitalisation process and on the condition that medical service resources remain basically unchanged, the quality and efficiency of medical services can be improved and hospitals' medical service revenue can be increased. Still others have studied the optimisation and reengineering of hospitals' outpatient processes, examination processes, and nursing processes.

Among the many medical service process improvement methods, Lean and Six Sigma approaches are increasingly drawing attention. The United States' Commonwealth Health Corporation (CHC) has used Six Sigma to save USD700,000 in hospital operating costs. The Netherlands' Red Cross implemented multiple Six Sigma projects, which have reduced the retention time of patients with chronic obstructive pulmonary disease (COPD) and reduced the number of patients using intravenous antibiotics. In China, Sichuan Huaxi Hospital, Shanghai General Hospital, and Zhejiang Taizhou Hospital have all carried out Lean and Six Sigma improvement projects. The effects of the application of the Lean and Six Sigma are primarily embodied in the following aspects: (1) process quality, such as improving outpatient diagnosis rate, reducing nosocomial infection rate, reducing medical malpractice, and so forth; (2) process efficiency, such as shortening patient examination waiting times and reducing the length of stay (LOS); (3) capacity of equipment, such as improving the scanning efficiency and service capacity of computed tomography (CT), magnetic resonance imaging (MRI), and positron-emission tomography (PET)-CT machines; (4) medical resources, such as improving the inventory management of pharmaceuticals and medical consumables; (5) employee and patient satisfaction, such as reducing employee overtime, optimising patient referral procedures, reducing report circulation time, reducing the pathology examination time, and so forth.

1.4.2 Medical Resource Allocation Management

The rational planning and allocation of medical service resources can significantly affect the efficiency of medical services. According to investigation: 80% of China's health resources are concentrated in urban areas and among them, 80% are allocated in large hospitals. A total of 64.8% of outpatients in provincial and municipal hospitals and 76.8% of patients hospitalised with chronic diseases can be treated in primary-care hospitals in their community. In many cases, patients with common illnesses can be treated in small and medium-sized hospitals, yet they are occupying beds and medical facilities in large hospitals and thus crowding out medical resources from patients with severe diseases. Since an excessive number of patients seek medical advice at large hospitals, the service quality of diagnoses and treatment at large hospitals is prone to decline. At the same time, few patients visit small and medium-sized hospitals. As a result, the economic performance of these small and medium-sized hospitals is too low to keep up normal operations.

Health resources are obviously scarce when compared with people's ever-growing health needs. Thus, the issue of the allocation and utilisation of health resources has become a primary problem for health management in many countries. The United States, the United Kingdom, Australia, the Netherlands, Germany, Belgium, France, Luxembourg, and other economically developed countries have shifted the focus of medical services to community families to increase outpatient medical service, and reduce hospital beds, cut down medical expenses as well.

The United Kingdom is a typical country in healthcare service management due to its implementation of the National Health Service (NHS). It takes the allocation and utilisation of health resources as an important part of its mission. Research institutions and governments at all levels have devoted significant amounts of research, inquiries, and practice to achieve the goal of fairness in the regional distribution of the NHS' resources and to determine standardised allocation methods. In 1975, the United States issued the *National Health Planning and Resources Development Act* (NHPRDA) and established a brand-new health planning management system to go along with it. The overall objective of this act was to achieve the reasonable allocation of facilities and resources in the health system. In Japan, based on its regional characteristics and health needs, the Japanese government has set up a three-tier medical care system. The first tier of the medical care system covers the administrative districts of the city, town, and village and relies primarily on clinics. The second tier covers the administrative districts of the metropolis, urban area, and prefecture and relies primarily on hospitals and receives referrals from the first tier. The third tier is primarily related to mental health, tuberculosis, and public health. When implementing regional health planning and resources allocating, Australia pays a significant amount of attention to the use of economic methods to carry out input-output analysis to meet its revenue goals for health investment. Singapore's medical service system is composed of public and private medical institutions. For primary healthcare services, doctors from the public or private systems can be visited, but if patients choose to see a doctor at a public hospital, they must be referred by a general clinic. At present, 80% of primary healthcare services are provided by private clinics and 20% are provided by public general clinics, while 80% of hospital services are provided by public hospitals and 20% are provided by private hospitals. The government subsidises residents seeking medical treatment at public medical institutions. In Chinese Hong Kong, regional health planning also starts with the hospital management mechanism, which focuses on optimising and reorganising medical resources. Hong Kong's healthcare is primarily funded by tax revenue, so the government shoulders the majority of health costs. The degree of government subsidies to public medical institutions is high and so residents' medical fees from public medical institutions are quite low, and the fairness of health services is relatively high. However, this health management model has also led to some problems. Therefore, governments have taken reform since the late 1980s to promote the consolidation of medical resources and cooperation between medical institutions.

At present, the most commonly used approaches for the allocation of health resources are health needs approach, service target approach, health resource/population ratio approach, and mathematical model approach. Besides, some other methods including Delphi method, preference investigation method (subjective probability method, opinion polling, etc.), can be utilised as well.

Generally speaking, the theoretical foundation for the allocation of health resources is basically based on the supply-and-demand analysis theory from the viewpoint of health economics. Sometimes, time-series models and statistical analysis methods are employed as well. Nowadays, these theoretical approaches and analysis technologies are still being improved continuously. More efforts should be devoted to the applications of computer and information technology, the extensive usage of database and big data analysis, and mathematical modelling.

In the future, it is still necessary to make use of operations research to explore on the demand forecasting and fairness study for health resource allocation so as to improve health planning efficiency, save planning costs, and formulate plans that meet current and future needs.

1.4.3 Application of Information Technology in Medical Services

Countries all over the world are increasingly aware that medical and health services can be remarkably promoted by the widespread adoption of modern health information technology (HIT) based on an electronic health record system (EHRS) and by finally connecting separate medical information systems into a modern healthcare information system (HIS). Doing so will also effectively deal with the impact of the explosive growth in medical knowledge and clinical information. Based upon this foundation, evolving towards 'smart medicine' is without a doubt the trend for medical services.

Broadly speaking, HIS refers to the integration of all information systems related to medical services. In a narrow sense, HIS is an information system for carrying out the comprehensive management and application of clinical data and knowledge. HIS has already gained widespread use and created positive social and economic effects. HIS can effectively increase the work efficiency of hospitals' medical staff. Meanwhile, it can achieve the goal of improving the quality of medical services by aiding and supporting the medical service process management.

HIS involves all aspects related to medical activities, including diagnosis, examination, treatment, pharmaceutical, and telemedicine information systems as well as clinical decision-making support systems. Among these, the objectives of the hospital management information system (HMIS) are to support hospitals' administrative management and transaction processing, to reduce the labour intensity, to help high-level leadership with decision-making, to improve hospitals' work efficiency, and to enable hospitals to provide greater social and economic benefits with less investment. The clinical information system (CIS) is an applied information system that takes electronic medical records as its core; collects laboratory, pathology, and decision support information together; and serves doctors and patients directly. The goals of the CIS are to support clinical activities, to collect and process patients' clinical information, to accumulate clinical medical knowledge, to improve the work efficiency of medical staff, and to provide patients with more, faster, and better service. The physician order processing, patient bedside, doctor workstation, and medication consultation systems all fall within the scope of the CIS. In a broader sense, picture archiving and communication system (PACs), laboratory information system (LIS), and telemedicine all are a part of the CIS.

The application of the HIS has tremendous value that is embodied specifically in the following facets: (1) Effectively reducing medical malpractice and negligence. A WHO research report shows that approximately one-third of patients die directly or indirectly due to irrational drug use. The clinical decision support system (CDSS) of a HIS can greatly improve doctors' level of rational drug use. Through electronic physician orders, electronic prescriptions, and a drug management information system, we can achieve the trifecta of doctor prescription, pharmacist review, and computer verification. This will, to a great extent, put a stop to the occurrence and use of irrational prescriptions and improve the quality of medical services. Meanwhile, the application of drug management information systems also reduces the probability of medication error in nursing process. (2) Alleviating the problem of expensive medical treatment. A HIS could realise the informatisation and standardisation of the medical examinations and tests, while the medical service information platform would enable information sharing between hospitals. As a result, patients could avoid repeated examinations and tests at different hospitals and thus reduce their medical expenses. At the same time, price supervision bureau, medical administration department, and insurance companies can also monitor irrational drug use and improper medical device use via HIS to render an institutional guarantee for economic medical treatments. (3) Improving the level and capabilities of medical services. A HIS can effectively improve the work efficiency of hospitals' medical staff and thus fulfil the needs of more patients. A HIS could provide the tracking of the entire process and dynamic management of patient information, which would simplify patient diagnosis and treatment, optimise the environment in which treatment is administered, and alleviate current shortcomings such as long queues and long waiting times. (4) Alleviating the medical disputes between physicians and patients. The public service platform based on HIS would ensure timely communication between physicians and patients and in between hospitals. It would also reduce many disputes caused by information asymmetry. (5) Relieving the high concentration problem of medical resources. Nowadays, in China, high-quality medical resources are primarily allocated to the large medical service institutions in big cities. The primary-care and community-based public health clinics should be strengthened urgently. Via the application of HIS and telemedicine technology, the current dearth of primary care medical resources can be mitigated, and the number of patient transfers to hospitals can be reduced, which will save a significant amount of medical fees while improving the level and capabilities of primary care medical services.

1.4.4   Medical Service Quality Management

At present, there are two representative concepts concerning the quality of medical services internationally. One is the official technology assessment (OTA) that was proposed in 1988: The quality of medical services refers to the degree by which patients expected results of medical service processes increase and their unexpected results decrease under current medical conditions via the use of the knowledge and technology of medicine and related sciences. The other representative concept was proposed by Donabedian in 1988: The quality of medical services refers to the ability to use reasonable methods (all aspects of medical services) to realise desired objectives (restoring patients' physical and mental health and satisfying the patients) [30]. Although the descriptions of these two concepts differ, they can both accurately express the key points of the concept of medical service quality: medical service quality is reflected in the degree to which medical services restore patients' physical and mental health and make patients satisfied.

The research on medical service quality indicators started earlier in the United States. In 1985, the Maryland Hospital Association established the International Quality Indicator Project (IQIP). In 1991, this assessment system was accepted internationally and become the largest medical quality indicator system in the world. IQIP has used an indicator assessment system that focuses on results and that utilises statistical, analytical, and data management methods to monitor medical quality to ensure the sustainability and stability of daily medical services. The European Office of the World Health Organisation has also proposed six assessment indicators: equality; improving health, reducing disease and its consequences; promoting healthy lifestyles; ensuring a healthy living environment; appropriate medical care; and knowledge development. Japan assesses medical service quality using six metrics: dynamic and static population indicators, average life expectancy, health status and treatment status, health-related issues, economic indicators, and manpower indicators.

As times have changed, medical service institutions have increasingly placed importance on the patient perspective in considering and investigating medical service quality, which reflects a patient-centred philosophy. For example, Coddington et al. have proposed that medical service quality should pay attention to the enthusiasm of service, medical staffs' technique and degree of specialisation, the availability of services, and the final outcomes of the medical treatments [31]. The Joint Commission on the Accreditation of Healthcare Organisations

(JCAHO) has proposed using nine metrics to assess medical service quality: efficacy, appropriateness, efficiency, respect and caring, safety, continuity, effectiveness, timeliness, and availability. Sower et al. have proposed the Key Quality Characteristics Assessment for Hospitals (KQCAH). They believe that hospitals' service quality can be assessed using such metrics as respect & caring, effectiveness and continuity, appropriateness, information, efficiency, and meals [32]. Finnish scholars Hiidenhovi et al. have proposed that medical service quality could be assessed using 12 questions, including information on course of treatment; compliance; professional skills; politeness; service awareness; test, drug, treatment plan, and disease development information; privacy protection; test efficiency; and overall treatment success rate [33].

Research in China on medical service quality indicators and assessment is deemed highly important. Some scholars have proposed using the ISO 9000 management philosophy to assess medical service quality. Some scholars have proposed four assessment metrics for medical service quality: overall hospital environment, medical service attitude, medical safety, and hospital administrative service measures. They have established a fuzzy comprehensive assessment method for evaluating medical service quality based on 19 indicators. Other scholars have also proposed assessing hospital service quality using metrics such as healing efficacy and side effects, quality of life, quality-adjusted life expectancy, cost-effectiveness ratio, appropriateness of treatment measures, and patient satisfaction. The patient satisfaction assessment is a method that scholars at home and abroad are fond of using to investigate medical service quality. The concept of patient satisfaction originated in research on customer satisfaction in marketing. At present, there does not exist a unified definition of patient satisfaction, though it does primarily include two aspects. The first is the value that medical services provide for patients, that is, the effects of the treatment on diseases and the recovery of patient health. These effects primarily come from the medical treatments supported by a wide variety of instruments and equipment. This is called explicit service satisfaction. The second is the feelings and experiences of the patients about the medical services they have received which is called implicit service satisfaction.

1.5   Main Contents and the Chapter Structure of This Book

Based on Chinese cases and the author's years of research findings, this book explores in detail multiple key issues in healthcare operations management from the perspective of the whole process of disease diagnosis and treatment chain. The related ideas, methods, and research results are organised in three stages: pre-hospital emergency care, in-hospital diagnosis and treatment, and post-hospital rehabilitation management.

The chapter structure for this book is as follows (Fig. 1.2):

Among them, the first stage is pre-hospital emergency care services. This is covered primarily in Chap. 2, which proposes research on the optimisation of the

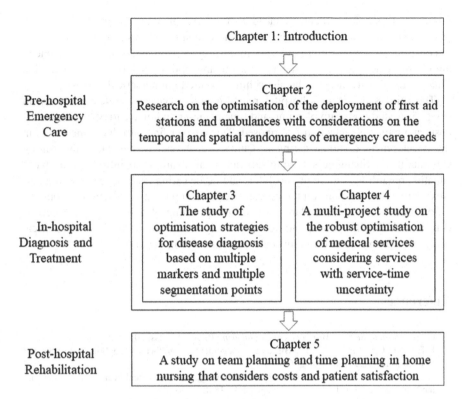

Pre-hospital
Emergency
Care

Chapter 1: Introduction

Chapter 2
Research on the optimisation of the deployment of first aid
stations and ambulances with considerations on the
temporal and spatial randomness of emergency care needs

In-hospital
Diagnosis and
Treatment

Chapter 3
The study of
optimisation strategies
for disease diagnosis
based on multiple
markers and multiple
segmentation points

Chapter 4
A multi-project study on
the robust optimisation
of medical services
considering services
with service-time
uncertainty

Post-hospital
Rehabilitation

Chapter 5
A study on team planning and time planning in home
nursing that considers costs and patient satisfaction

Fig. 1.2 The chapter structure of this book

deployment of first aid stations and ambulances with considerations on the temporal and spatial randomness of emergency care needs. This chapter first details the characteristics of the temporal and spatial randomness of emergency care needs and then establishes the ways in which the function of randomness is expressed to provide a data-based and technical foundation for research on the optimal allocation of emergency care resources. Upon this foundation, the optimisation of first aid station layout and ambulance deployment are studied. The numerical analysis and effect validation of the model and algorithm are then conducted based on the real emergency medical service data collected from Songjiang district, Shanghai.

The second stage is in-hospital diagnosis and treatment services, which are covered primarily in Chaps. 3 and 4. In Chap. 3, the study of optimisation strategies for disease diagnosis based on multiple markers and multiple segmentation points is proposed. First, the traditional diagnostic methods and the ways to evaluate the diagnostic accuracy of colorectal cancer and its tumour markers are introduced. Upon this foundation, a tumour diagnostic method based on multiple markers and multiple segmentation points using fuzzy rough set theory is designed. The effectiveness of this method is verified on empirical data. In Chap. 4, a multi-project robust optimisation of medical services considering service-time uncertainty is proposed. First, the difficulties faced in the time planning of multiple medical projects are introduced. Then, the stochastic dynamic optimisation theory is used to construct an optimisation model for multi-project planning. Thereafter, a genetic algorithm is designed and used to find out the optimal solution for the model. Finally, the effectiveness of the algorithm is verified via numerical analysis.

The third stage is post-hospital rehabilitation services, covered primarily in Chap. 5. A study on team planning and time planning in home caring that considers costs and patient satisfaction is proposed. This chapter first introduces the trends in the development of home caring in China and abroad. It then takes the Anting Community in Shanghai's Jiading District as an example to introduce the basic situation regarding community hospitals and home caring needs in this community. Next, with considerations on the operating costs and patient satisfaction, an optimisation model for the team planning and time planning of home caring services is constructed. Finally, corresponding solution algorithms are derived, and numerical analysis of problems of different scales is conducted in depth.

References

1. Q. Su, *Medical Service Management Engineering* (Science Press, 2014)
2. P.T. Chen, C.L. Lin, W.N. Wu, Big data management in healthcare: adoption challenges and implications. Int. J. Inf. Manag. (2020)
3. Z.J. Wu, V. Trigo, Impact of information system integration on the healthcare management and medical services. Int. J. Healthc. Manag. **14**(4), 1348–1356 (2021)
4. Y. Xie, L. Lu, F. Gao, S.J. He, et al., Integration of artificial intelligence, blockchain, and wearable technology for chronic disease management: a new paradigm in smart healthcare. Curr. Med. Sci. **41**(6), 1123–1133 (2021)
5. T. Lang, Advancing global health research through digital technology and sharing data. Science **331**(6018), 714–717 (2011)
6. V.J. Powell, A. Acharya, Disease prevention: data integration. Science (New York, N.Y.) **338**(6112), 1285 (2012)
7. C.L. Ireson, Critical pathways: effectiveness in achieving patient outcomes. J. Nurs. Adm. **27**(6), 16–23 (1997)
8. A.O. Berg, D. Atkins, W. Tierney, Clinical practice guidelines in practice and education. J. Gen. Intern. Med. **12**(2), S25–S33 (1997)
9. D.B. Pryor, D.F. Fortin, Managing the delivery of health care: care-plans/managed care/practice guidelines. Int. J. Biomed. Comput. **39**(1), 105–109 (1995)
10. K.J. Zehe, P.B. Dawson, S.C. Yang, Standardized clinical care pathways for major thoracic cases reduce hospital costs. Ann. Thorac. Surg. **66**(3), 914–917 (1998)
11. L. Winterberg, Quality improvement in healthcare. Ann. Qual. Congr. Transac., 352–353 (2001)
12. J.X. Hong, Developing clinical pathways that can improve medical quality. For. Med. Sci. Manag. **73**(3), 23 (2002)
13. M.N. Li, S.Z. Li, Effective way of comprehensively increasing medical quality: clinical pathway. J. Nurs. Sci. **18**(3), 84–85 (2003)
14. Y.B. Liu, Y. Sun, X.W. Li, Implementing of clinical pathways for assuring quality of health care and lowering medical expenses. Chin. Hosp. **6**, 39–40 (2002)
15. H.J. Zhang, S.M. Tong, J. Song, et al., Probe into clinical therapeutic measure of some Angiocardiopathy cases. Chin. J. Pract. Nurs. **19**(5), 65–65 (2003)

16. D.J. Ogilvie-Harris, D.J. Botsford, R.W. Hawker, Elderly patients with hip fractures: improved outcome with the use of care maps with high-quality medical and nursing protocols. J. Orthop. Trauma **7**(5), 428–437 (1993)

17. M. Panella, S. Marchisio, A. Barbieri, et al., A cluster randomized trial to assess the impact of clinical pathways for patients with stroke: rationale and design of the clinical pathways for effective and appropriate care study [NCT00673491]. BMC Health Serv. Res. **8**(1), 223 (2008)

18. S.R. Preston, S.R. Markar, C.R. Baker, et al., Impact of a multidisciplinary standardized clinical pathway on perioperative outcomes in patients with oesophageal cancer. Br. J. Surg. **100**(1), 105–112 (2013)

19. L. Stead, C. Arthur, A. Cleary, Do multidisciplinary pathways of care affect patient satisfaction? Health Care Risk Rep., 13–15 (1995)

20. P.A. van Dam, G. Verheyden, A. Sugihara, et al., A dynamic clinical pathway for the treatment of patients with early breast cancer is a tool for better cancer care: implementation and prospective analysis between 2002–2010. World J. Surg. Oncol. **11**, 70 (2013)

21. J.G. Williams, R. Roberts, M.J. Rigby, Integrated patient records: another move towards quality for patients? Qual. Health Care **2**(2), 73–74 (1993)

22. C. Mosher, P. Cronk, A. Kidd, et al., Upgrading practice with critical pathways. Am. J. Nurs. **92**(1), 41–44 (1992)

23. P. Brunings, L. van de Laar, et al., Evaluation of an adverse outcome index for the quality of obstetric care delivered by multidisciplinary care chains. Int. J. Integr. Care **13**(5), 1–2 (2013)

24. Z. Wang, M.X. Chen, et al., Effectiveness of optimised care chain for hip fractures in elderly Chinese. Int. J. Health Plann. Manag. **36**(5), 1445–1464 (2021)

25. G.B. Yang, X.M. Yi, et al., The explore and action of the mode in special disease based on the chain of diagnoses and treatment. Chin. Hosp. Manag. **27**(9), 69–70 (2007)

26. R. Qiu, Editorial—We must rethink service encounters. Serv. Sci. **5**(1), 1–3 (2013)

27. G. Svensson, New aspects of research into service encounters and service quality. Int. J. Serv. Ind. Manag. **17**(3), 245–257 (2006)

28. C. Gainty, Mr. Gilbreth's motion pictures—the evolution of medical efficiency. N. Engl. J. Med. **374**(2), 109–111 (2016)

29. E. Lee-Lewandrowski, D. Corboy, K. Lewandrowski, J. Sinclair, S. McDermot, T.I. Benzer, Implementation of a point-of-care satellite laboratory in the emergency department of an academic medical center. Impact on test turnaround time and patient emergency department length of stay. Arch. Pathol. Lab. Med. **127**(4), 456–460 (2003)

30. A. Donabedian, The quality of care. How can it be assessed? J. Am. Med. Assoc. **260**(12), 1743–1748 (1988)

31. D.C. Coddington, K.D. Moore, Quality of care as a business strategy. Healthc. Forum **30**(2), 29–32 (1987)

32. V. Sower, J. Duffy, W. Kilbourne, G. Kohers, P. Jones, The dimensions of service quality for hospitals: development and use of the KQCAH scale. Health Care Manag. Rev. **26**(2), 47–59 (2001)

33. H. Hiidenhovi, K. Nojonen, P. Laippala, Measurement of outpatients' views of service quality in a Finnish University Hospital. J. Adv. Nurs. **38**(1), 59–67 (2002)

Chapter 2
Research on the Optimal Deployment of First Aid Stations and Ambulances Considering the Temporal and Spatial Stochasticity of Demand

Timeliness of responses is a key indicator for evaluating emergency medical services (EMS). The goal of ambulance allocation is to ensure that there is a sufficient level of demand coverage, which is usually expressed as the amount of coverage as a percentage of total demand. McCormack and Coates pointed out that the basis of optimising ambulance allocation is the distribution of the EMS demand, and the generation process of the EMS demand is a complex stochastic process [1].

Existing studies of the specific spatial locations of EMS demand still fall short in terms of research depth. One of the major reasons is that ambulance allocation research is usually conducted based on city map, in which the spatially distributed demand that may arise anytime and anywhere is abstracted into certain representative points on map. Although some recent studies have attempted to split the entire space under planning into a series of rectangular grids, the stochastic spatial distribution of demand still cannot be precisely described using this approach.

With the accumulation of EMS data, accurately describing the stochastic distribution of EMS demand is now possible. In this study, we will analyse and describe the stochasticity of EMS demand in two dimensions: the spatial distribution of demand (spatial dimension) and the variation in the quantity of demand over time (temporal dimension). Furthermore, considering the spatiotemporal stochasticity of demand, the location problem of the first aid stations and the allocation problem of ambulance are explored systematically. To these ends, the optimisation models are proposed and the corresponding algorithms are developed. Meanwhile, the real EMS service data collected in Songjiang district, Shanghai, are utilised to verify the effectiveness of the models and algorithms.

Q. Su, *Healthcare Operations Management*, SpringerBriefs in Service Science, https://doi.org/10.1007/978-3-031-13397-8_2

2.1 Quantitative Description and Analysis of Spatiotemporal Stochasticity of Demand for Emergency Medical Services

2.1.1 Stochasticity of EMS Demand in the Spatial Dimension

The geographic distribution of EMS demand shows strong stochasticity. Figure 2.1 depicts the geographic distribution of EMS demand in the Songjiang district of Shanghai in 2013 and 2014; the dots represent the EMS demand, and the symbol H represents the allocation of ambulance stations. The data analysis indicates that the demand for EMS services is denser in the centres of cities, towns, and communities and more scattered in peripheral areas.

Usually, in the current research works, the spatial spread EMS demands are simplified into a number of concentrated demand points located in the subareas (towns or communities) of the district. And the administrative centre of the town or community is used to denote the spatial location of the corresponding demands. This overly simplified approach cannot represent the stochasticity of the spatial distribution of the EMS demand. Therefore, some scholars have proposed the use of a grid system that divides the entire space into a number of rectangular areas (Fig. 2.2). Each rectangular area will be regarded as a demand point.

Taking Songjiang district in Shanghai as an example, the total area of the district is 605.64 square kilometres. If we use 2 km × 2 km^2 to split the area, the district can be divided into 187 demand points as shown in Fig. 2.2.

The two approaches discussed above neglect an essential characteristic of EMS demand. Demand is usually more densely concentrated in urban areas, where there is a larger population, and more scattered in peripheral areas. The distribution of demand across different communities is independent. Hence, it is necessary to overcome the shortcomings in the traditional regional division approaches. Based

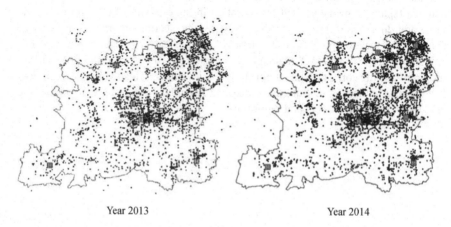

Year 2013   Year 2014

Fig. 2.1 Distribution of EMS demands in Songjiang District, Shanghai, 2013–2014

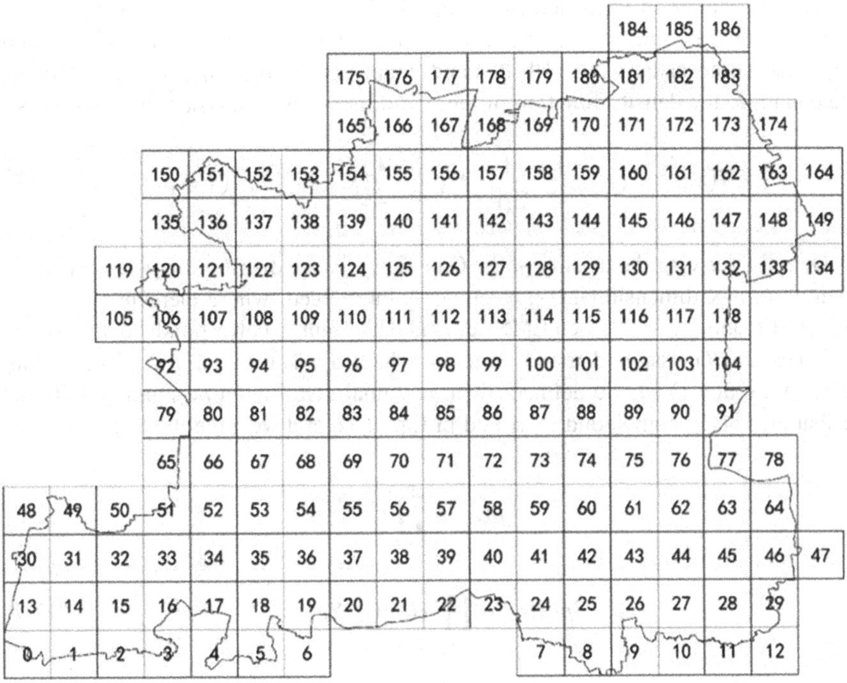

Fig. 2.2 Diagram of the grid demand for Songjiang District

on the distribution pattern and characteristics of EMS demand, the Gaussian mixture model is utilised to quantitatively describe the spatial distribution of demand.

McLachlan and Peel found that any complex form of distribution can be approximated through a mixture of multiple Gaussian distributions [2]. Therefore, in this work, Gaussian mixture model clustering method is employed to divide spatially distributed EMS demand into multiple Gaussian demand zones. Thereby, the stochasticity of the EMS demand can be accurately described and quantitatively analysed.

The Gaussian mixture distribution can be regarded as the linear superposition of a series of Gaussian distributions [3]. Assuming EMS demand in an area under planning consists of K Gaussian distributions, then the probability density function of the mixture model is

$$p(\mathbf{x}) = \sum_{k=1}^{K} \pi_k N(\mathbf{x}|\mu_k, \ \Sigma_k) \tag{2.1}$$

In Eq. (2.1), $\mathbf{x}$ denotes a two-dimensional random variable that is formed by the latitude and longitude coordinates; π_k is the mixing coefficient, which is the probability of each set of Gaussian distributions being selected or the probability that demand will arise in each demand zone; $N(x|\mu_k, \Sigma_k)$ denotes the density of each Gaussian distribution, where μ_k denotes the average values of the latitude and longitude coordinates of the kth demand zone; and Σ_k is a covariance matrix. In the equation, the density function of the two-dimensional Gaussian distribution is

$$N(x|\mu_k, \Sigma_k) = \frac{1}{2\pi} \frac{1}{|\Sigma_k|^{1/2}} \exp\left\{-\frac{1}{2}(x - \mu_k)^T \Sigma_k^{-1}(x - \mu_k)\right\} \tag{2.2}$$

Directly deriving the density of the Gaussian mixture distribution $p(x)$ is difficult. Therefore, a K-dimensional 0–1 vector z is introduced, where element z_i satisfies $z_i \in \{0, 1\}$, and $\sum_i z_i = 1$. Each EMS demand data point x_n corresponds to a z_n, which indicates the Gaussian demand zone in which x_n is located. As such, a joint distribution $p(x, z)$ can be defined; then, marginal distribution $p(z)$ and conditional probability $p(x|z)$ correspond to π_k and in Eq. (2.1), and we have the following:

$$p(z) = \prod_{k=1}^{K} \pi_k^{z_k} \tag{2.3}$$

$$p(x|z) = \prod_{k=1}^{K} N(x|\mu_k, \Sigma_k)^{z_k} \tag{2.4}$$

Meanwhile, according to the rules of addition and multiplication, we have

$$p(x) = \sum_z p(z)p(x|z) = \sum_{k=1}^{K} \pi_k N(x|\mu_k, \Sigma_k) \tag{2.5}$$

In data clustering, a set of parameters is given to calculate the probability that a data point belongs to a Gaussian area; this way, EMS demand is attributed to different areas, and each Gaussian area's mean and covariance are estimated through reiteration. Meanwhile, when new EMS demand arises, there is a need to know the probability that the demand belongs to each Gaussian distribution to determine the area to which the new demand belongs. This probability can be calculated using Bayes' theorem:

$$p(z_k = 1|x_n) = \frac{p(z_k = 1)p(x_n|z_k = 1)}{\sum_{j=1}^{K} p(z_j = 1)p(x_n|z_j = 1)} = \frac{\pi_k N(x_n|\mu_k, \Sigma_k)}{\sum_{j=1}^{K} \pi_j N(x_n|\mu_j, \Sigma_j)} \tag{2.6}$$

In evaluating data fitness, the maximum log-likelihood function is employed [4]:

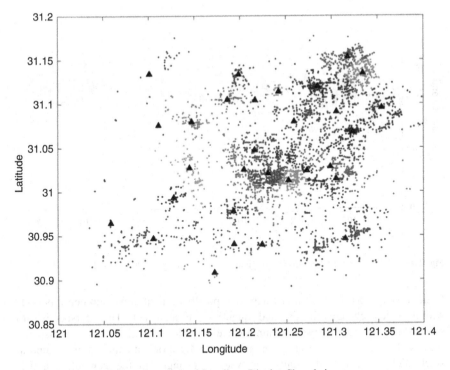

Fig. 2.3 EMS demand clustering result of Songjiang District, Shanghai

$$E = \ln p(\mathbf{x}|\pi, \ \mu, \ \Sigma) = \sum_{n=1}^{N} \ln \left[\sum_{k=1}^{K} \pi_k N(\mathbf{x}_n|\mu_k, \ \Sigma_k) \right] \qquad (2.7)$$

Using the EMS data of Songjiang District, Shanghai, we obtained the data clustering result as shown in Fig. 2.3. A total of 30 Gaussian demand zones were obtained. The points with the same colour represent the EMS demand in the same area, and the black triangles represent the cluster centroid points of the demand zones.

2.1.2 Stochasticity of EMS Demand in the Temporal Dimension

Stochasticity of EMS demand in the temporal dimension refers to the random fluctuations in the demand quantity over time. In the existing literature, the temporal stochasticity of EMS demand is usually classified into two perspectives as short-term stochasticity and long-term stochasticity. The short-term perspective focuses on the daily operations of ambulances, namely, the short-term stochasticity of demand.

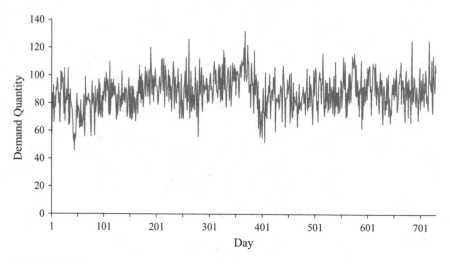

Fig. 2.4 EMS demand fluctuations in Songjiang District, Shanghai, 2013–2014

Under this approach, the 24 h of a day are typically divided into a number of periods within which changes in demand quantity are analysed. This perspective to stochasticity is usually used in ambulance redeployment and dynamic dispatch studies. In long-term planning for ambulance location and allocation, temporal stochasticity refers to the daily (or weekly) changes in the demand quantity. Research on this issue attempts to derive demand distribution patterns from the ongoing daily or weekly changes in demand. Most studies agree that as long as the probability distribution of the change in demand quantity can be derived, the stochastic programming problem that involves stochastic demand can be solved by being converted to deterministic decision-making problem [5]. Notably, some studies argue that other methods may be required when there is limited historical data or the distribution of the random variable is complex. For instance, Ng et al. proposed a 'distribution-free' approach to process the randomly changing demand [6].

In China's first-tier cities, such as Beijing and Shanghai, data collection and entry for EMS demand have become routine. Specialised EMS information systems are used to help dispatchers record and store relevant data. Furthermore, changes in urban infrastructure and population are usually slow. As such, the assumptions made in this study about the temporal stochasticity of EMS demand are similar to those of most research, i.e., the probability distribution of the random fluctuations in the demand quantity can be derived via statistical analysis of historical data.

From a long-term perspective, Fig. 2.4 shows the changes in EMS demand quantity in Songjiang District, Shanghai, during the 730 days of 2013 and 2014; the daily demand quantity randomly fluctuates between 40 and 140. Visually, no significant increase in demand can be identified over the 2 years. In 2014, the total EMS demand was 32,409, only 651 more than in 2013.

Figure 2.5 shows the result of the probability distribution fitting performed for the 2 years of EMS data. Within the administrative boundaries of Songjiang District,

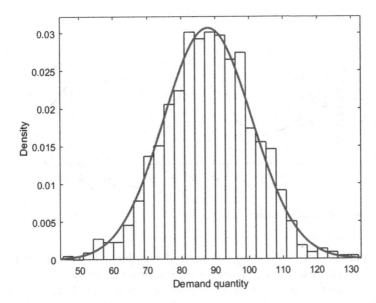

Fig. 2.5 EMS demand quantity distribution fitting

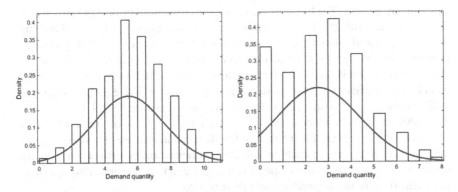

Fig. 2.6 Examples of the result of demand quantity distribution fitting

Shanghai, the daily EMS demand follows the normal distribution with a mean of 87.9 and standard deviation of 13; the mean squared error is 0.000746. A Kolmogorov–Smirnov test is then performed for the demand distribution fitting; at a 95% confidence level, the P value is 0.836. The hypothesis test result demonstrates that the random fluctuations in the EMS demand quantity can be regarded as a normal distribution.

A similar demand stochasticity analysis can be performed for the 30 demand zones obtained through data clustering using the Gaussian mixture model in the previous section. The results indicate that the normal distribution hypothesis is accepted for 23 of the 30 zones; the other seven areas have an inferior fitting mainly because demand is low, and the random fluctuations are significant. Figure 2.6

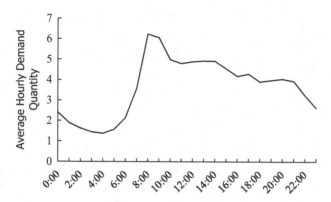

Fig. 2.7 Changes in demand quantity over 24 h

presents one area with good fitting and one with poor fitting as examples of the test result. Although the fitting of a number of areas is somewhat inferior, the trend in the changes is similar. As such, this study still posits that the demand fluctuations in each zone approximate a normal distribution.

From the short-term perspective, Fig. 2.7 shows the average hourly demand of the 24 h in a day in 2013. The figure indicates that the changes in the demand arrival rate are significant, with the highest demand almost five times the lowest. Previous research has usually divided the 24 h into several time periods to simplify consideration of the changes in the EMS demand arrival rate. Under this approach, an average arrival rate is calculated for each time period, which is then input into the model for ambulance dispatch or relocation optimisation. For example, Bélanger et al. set every 2 h as a time period for demand arrival statistics [7]. Lam et al. and Schneeberger have conducted similar research [8, 9]. To a certain extent, this approach may reflect the fluctuations in the demand arrival rate. However, due to the relatively long time in each period, the description of the arrival rate is quite rough. To enhance ambulance dispatch performance, a more accurate description of the fluctuations of the demand arrival rate is needed.

2.2   Location Selection for Ambulance Stations Considering Spatiotemporal Stochasticity of Demand

In optimising ambulance allocation, location selection for ambulance stations must first be considered from a long-term perspective to maximise the demand coverage provided by the stations. At this stage, the number of ambulances for each station is not considered. To prevent the scenario in which the primary station (the station nearest to the demand zone) does not have ambulances for dispatch and help must be requested from stations in other zones, which often occurs in the real world, this study draws from the dual coverage model and allocates a standby station for each demand zone.

2.2.1 Problem Description

The coverage problem refers to how to maximise the coverage of demand with the limited ambulance stations given the service radius which is determined by the service response time requirement. Different from previous studies, this study proposes a multi-station coverage planning model with tiers of priorities. In this model, each demand zone is provided with a list of ambulance stations, and each station on the list has cascading coverage radiuses. (For instance, a station with first-tier priority covers an area with a radius of 12 min of driving, and a station with second-tier priority covers an area with a radius of 15 min of driving). Under this arrangement, even if there are no ambulances available in the first-tier station, the zone can be served by the second-tier station in a timely manner.

The main assumptions in the location selection model are as follows:

1. Each demand zone has one and only one primary station that provides the first-tier priority service.
2. Each demand zone has one and only one standby station to provide the second-tier priority service (backup services) to the zone. The distance of the standby station to the demand point is larger than that of the primary station.
3. Based on the data analysis in Sect. 2.1.2, it is assumed that the weekly demand for EMS follows the normal distribution.

2.2.2 Model Construction

Explanations of symbols:

α_{ij}: 0–1 decision variable—if station j is the primary station for demand zone i, $\alpha_{ij} = 1$; otherwise $\alpha_{ij} = 0$

β_{ij}: 0–1 decision variable—if station j is the standby station for demand zone i, $\beta_{ij} = 1$; otherwise $\beta_{ij} = 0$

x_j: 0–1 variable—if candidate station j is used, $x_j = 1$; otherwise $x_j = 0$

K: the set of demand zones

M: the set of candidate stations

W: the set of stations that are used

d_i: demand quantity generated in demand zone i, $d_i \sim N(\mu_{di}, \sigma_{di})$

t_{ij}: the driving time from station j to demand zone i; when the spatial stochasticity of demand is taken into account, t_{ij} is a random variable

t_{sr}: the ideal driving time from the primary station to the demand zone

t_{s1}: the maximum driving time required from the primary station to the demand zone
t_{s2}: the maximum driving time required from the standby station to the demand zone

The objective function is to minimise the number of stations used:

$$\min f = \sum_{j \in M} x_j \tag{2.8}$$

The model needs to satisfy the following constraints:

$$\sum_{i \in K} \left(d_i \cdot \sum_{j \in M} \left(\Pr\left(t_{ij} \le t_{sr}\right) \cdot \alpha_{ij} \right) \right) \ge \varphi \sum_{i \in K} d_i \tag{2.9}$$

$$\sum_{j \in M} t_{ij} \alpha_{ij} \le t_{s1}, \forall i \in K \tag{2.10}$$

$$\sum_{j \in M} t_{ij} \beta_{ij} \le t_{s2}, \forall i \in K \tag{2.11}$$

$$\sum_{j \in M} \alpha_{ij} = 1, \forall i \in K \tag{2.12}$$

$$\sum_{j \in M} \beta_{ij} = 1, \forall i \in K \tag{2.13}$$

$$\sum_{j \in M} \alpha_{ij} x_j = 1, \ \forall i \in K \tag{2.14}$$

$$\sum_{j \in M} \beta_{ij} x_j = 1, \ \forall i \in K \tag{2.15}$$

$$\alpha_{ij} + \beta_{ij} \le 1, \ \forall i \in K, j \in M \tag{2.16}$$

$$\sum_{j \in W} \alpha_{ij} \bar{t}_{ij} \le \bar{t}_{im}, \ \forall m \in W, \forall i \tag{2.17}$$

Constraint (2.9) corresponds to a classic constraint in the location selection problem for ambulance stations; it is expected that φ percent of the demand can be served by the primary station within time t_{sr}; in the constraint, $\Pr(t_{ij} \le t_{sr})$ denotes the probability that the driving time from station j to demand point i is shorter than standard time t_{sr}. Generally, time t_{sr} is less than the driving time needed for the coverage radius of the station. This constraint is commonly used by government departments to evaluate the performance of EMS centres. For instance, the standard coverage radius for ambulance stations in Shanghai is 12 min of driving distance, while the government may hope that 60% of demand can be served more promptly, e.g., within 7 min. Constraints (2.10) and (2.11) require that the driving time required from the primary station and the standby station to the demand zone that they serve will not exceed the pre-set standard coverage time, t_{s1} and t_{s2}, respectively. Constraints (2.12) and (2.13) require that each demand zone has one and only one primary station and standby station, respectively. Constraints (2.14) and (2.15) ensure that when station j is used as a primary or standby station, $x_j = 1$. Constraint (2.16) ensures that the primary and standby stations of a demand zone are not the same station. Constraint (2.17) indicates that the distance from each demand zone to its primary station should be shorter than the distance to the standby station, and $\bar{t}$ denotes the average driving time.

In the model, constraints (2.9), (2.10), and (2.11) contain random demand quantity d and driving time t_{ij}. The randomness of the driving time is due to the randomness of the specific spatial location where the demand is generated. To solve this stochastic model, the random constraints must be converted into corresponding deterministic constraints.

2.2.3   Treatment of Random Variables

This study employs the chance-constrained programming method to solve the model. First, constraints (2.9), (2.10), and (2.11), which contain random variables, are expressed in the chance-constrained form:

$$\Pr\left(\sum_{i \in K}\left(d_i \cdot \sum_{j \in M}\left(\Pr\left(t_{ij} \le t_{sr}\right) \cdot \alpha_{ij}\right)\right) \ge \varphi \sum_{i \in K} d_i\right) \ge 1 - \theta_1 \qquad (2.18)$$

$$\Pr\left(t_{s1} - \sum_{j \in M} t_{ij}\alpha_{ij} \ge 0\right) \ge 1 - \theta_2 \qquad (2.19)$$

$$\Pr\left(t_{s2} - \sum_{j \in M} t_{ij}\beta_{ij} \ge 0\right) \ge 1 - \theta_3 \qquad (2.20)$$

in which, θ_1, θ_2, and θ_3 are risk parameters. Formula (2.18) indicates the probability that constraint "φ percent demand can be served by the primary station within t_{sr} time" can be satisfied is $1 - \theta_1$. Formulas (2.19) and (2.20) indicate that the probability that constraints "the driving time required from the primary station and the standby station to the demand zone that they serve will not exceed the pre-set standard coverage time, t_{s1} and t_{s2}, respectively" can be satisfied is $1 - \theta_2$ and $1 - \theta_3$, respectively.

First, we consider the impact of the stochasticity of demand in constraint (2.18). As the demand quantity follows the normal distribution, this study establishes the analytical relationship between the demand quantity and the constraint risk probability through the cumulative distribution function for a normal distribution. This method of conversion draws inspiration from the conversion method of nonlinear constraints in linear conic optimisation [10]. In accordance with the probability distribution function of the normal distribution, the constraint can be converted to the following form:

$$
\Phi^{-1}(\theta_1)\sqrt{\sum_{i\in K}\left(\sum_{j\in M}(\Pr(t_{ij}\leq t_{sr})\cdot \alpha_{ij})-\varphi\right)^2 \sigma_{di}^2}
$$

$$
-\sum_{i\in K}\mu_{di}\left(\sum_{j\in M}(\Pr(t_{ij}\leq t_{sr})\cdot \alpha_{ij})\right)
$$

$$
\leq 0 \tag{2.21}
$$

Next, the issue of spatial stochasticity, namely, $\Pr(t_{ij}\leq t_{sr})$ in the above formula, must be addressed. Let u_i and v_i be the latitude and longitude coordinates of the demand in the ith demand zone, respectively, and they follow a two-dimensional Gaussian distribution $f_i(u_i, v_i)$; let u_j and v_j be the latitude and longitude coordinates of the jth station; and let V be the speed of the ambulance. To measure the distance between two points, this study uses the Manhattan distance, which researchers believe is more appropriate when studying urban transportation issues [11]. The constraint is further converted to a certainty form, as follows:

$$
\Phi^{-1}(\theta_1)\sqrt{\sum_{i\in K}\left(\sum_{j\in M}\left(\iint\limits_{|u_i-u_j|+|v_i-v_j|\leq V\cdot t_{sr}} f_i(u_i, v_i)du_idv_i\cdot \alpha_{ij}\right)-\varphi\right)^2 \sigma_{di}^2}
$$

$$
-\sum_{i\in K}\mu_{di}\left(\sum_{j\in M}\left(\iint\limits_{|u_i-u_j|+|v_i-v_j|\leq V\cdot t_{sr}} f_i(u_i, v_i)du_idv_i\cdot \alpha_{ij}\right)\right)\leq 0 \tag{2.22}
$$

In the formula,

$$
f_i(u_i, v_i) = \frac{1}{2\pi\sigma_{iu}\sigma_{iv}\sqrt{1-\rho_i^2}}
$$

$$
\exp\left(-\frac{1}{2(1-\rho_i^2)}\left(\frac{(u_i-\mu_{iu})^2}{\sigma_{iu}^2}+\frac{(v_i-\mu_{iv})^2}{\sigma_{iv}^2}-\frac{2\rho_i(u_i-\mu_{iu})(v_i-\mu_{iv})}{\sigma_{iu}\sigma_{iv}}\right)\right) \tag{2.23}
$$

The double integral in formula (2.22) calculates the probability that the driving time from each station to each demand point is below t_{sr}; μ_{iu} and μ_{iv} are the average values of the latitude and longitude coordinates of the demand points in the ith demand zone; σ_{iu} and σ_{iv} are standard deviations; and ρ_i is the correlation coefficient. The values of these variables can be obtained from the data clustering using the Gaussian mixture model, as discussed previously. Similar to constraint (2.21), constraints (2.19) and (2.20) can be further expressed in a certainty form:

$$\sum_{j \in M} \iint_{|u_i-u_j|+|v_i-v_j| \leq V \cdot t_{s1}} f_i(u_i, v_i) du_i dv_i \cdot \alpha_{ij} \geq 1 - \theta_2 \tag{2.24}$$

$$\sum_{j \in M} \iint_{|u_i-u_j|+|v_i-v_j| \leq V \cdot t_{s2}} f(u_i, v_i) du_i dv_i \cdot \beta_{ij} \geq 1 - \theta_3 \tag{2.25}$$

By replacing constraints (2.9), (2.10), and (2.11) in the original programming problem with constraints (2.22), (2.24), and (2.25), the stochastic programming problem is converted to a quadratic constraint programming problem.

2.2.4 Case Analysis and Discussion

In this work, the operations data of the EMS centre in Songjiang District, Shanghai, is utilised to verify the effectiveness of the stochastic model in location selection of ambulance stations. To expend the feasible solution spaces, besides eight existing ambulance stations in the Songjiang District, seven big hospitals are added as candidate ambulance stations. The location of the 15 candidate stations is shown in Fig. 2.8. The symbols ⊞ denote the current existing ambulance stations, the red crosses represent the newly added candidate stations, and the triangles represent the cluster centroid points of the 30 demand zones.

The assigned values for the location selection model's parameters are shown in Table 2.1. The value assignments for t_s and t_{s1} are based on past similar research [12], and the value assignment for t_{s2} is based on infrastructure regulations in Shanghai.

Based on the spatiotemporal scholastic model and its digital calculation, the optimal location plan for ambulance station is derived as shown in Fig. 2.9. The points encircled by the dotted lines are the selected stations. The new plan uses nine ambulance stations, including five existing and four newly added stations.

Using 2014 EMS operations data, a simulation analysis is conducted to verify the new plan's operational performance, and the results are presented in Table 2.2. The operational performance of the current plan is also simulated and listed as the baseline for comparison. As the stochastic model limits the maximum driving time from the primary station to the demand zone to 12 min, the time delay in Table 2.2 refers to the driving time that exceeds the 12-min limit.

Table 2.2 indicates that although the location selection plan produced by the spatiotemporal stochastic model requires one more station than the existing plan,

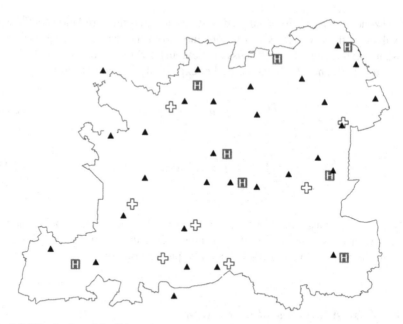

Fig. 2.8 Distribution of feasible stations and cluster centroid points of demand zones

Table 2.1 Assigned parameter values for the location selection model

Parameter	Value
$|K|$	30
$|M|$	15
t_{sr}	7 min
t_{s1}	12 min
t_{s2}	20 min
φ	0.6
θ_1	0.1
θ_2	0.1
θ_3	0.1

overall performance under the new plan is significantly improved through station location optimisation. The average response time is reduced by 3 min, with very few delays.

Furthermore, three different scenarios are considered and the corresponding model is designed and verified digitally to compare the results of optimisation: (1) the spatiotemporal stochastic model, which takes into account the demand quantity and spatial stochasticity; (2) the spatial stochastic model, which only considers the spatial stochasticity of the demand and where the temporal stochasticity is replaced by the average demand quantity; and (3) the average demand quantity model, which does not consider the stochasticity and where the stochastic demand quantity and stochastic distribution of demand locations are

Fig. 2.9 Station allocation plan derived by the spatiotemporal stochastic model

Table 2.2 Performance of location plan based on spatiotemporal stochastic model

	No. of stations	Average response time	Average weekly delay time	Average weekly times of delay
Plan based on spatiotemporal stochastic model	9	7.20 min	0.66 min	1.8
Existing plan	8	10.45 min	72.69 min	26.0

Table 2.3 Results of comparison test

Model	No. of stations	Average response time	Average weekly delay time	Average weekly times of delay
Average demand quantity model	7	9.60 min	36.92 min	24.0
Spatial stochastic model	8	8.25 min	5.93 min	5.1
Spatiotemporal stochastic model	9	7.20 min	0.66 min	1.8
Existing plan	8	10.45 min	72.69 min	26.0

replaced by the average demand quantity. The results of the comparison are presented in Table 2.3.

The results in Table 2.3 indicate that as the average demand quantity model neglects the impact of the spatiotemporal stochasticity of the demand, it produces an optimistic plan in which seven stations would be able to meet the demand. However,

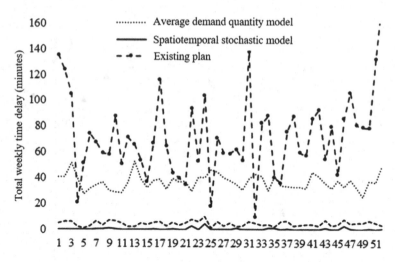

Fig. 2.10 Comparison of total weekly delay time

the simulation test using real operations data indicates that many times of EMS delay occur. To ensure the effectiveness of the EMS network, the spatial stochastic model employs more stations, and the average EMS delay time is reduced accordingly. Although both the spatial stochastic model and the existing allocation plan use eight stations, the geographic allocation of the eight stations is different from each other. The results produced by the spatial stochastic model are apparently superior to those produced by the existing allocation plan in terms of response time, delay time, and times of delay, indicating that the location selection plan generated by the spatial stochastic model is more scientific and effective.

Figures 2.10 and 2.11 compare the EMS delay time and times of delay in 2014 under each model, respectively.

Figures 2.10 and 2.11 show that when the chance-constrained programming model, which takes into account the stochasticity of the spatial distribution of demand, is employed for the optimisation, the results are apparently superior to those produced by the average demand quantity model or the existing plan, as evidenced by the significant difference in the time delay and the number of delays. When the stochasticity of the demand quantity and stochasticity of spatial distribution are considered simultaneously, the effect is slightly better than that when only the spatial stochasticity of demand is taken into account. However, because the results produced by the spatial stochastic model are already very good, the improvement in the spatiotemporal stochastic model is limited.

Referring to constraint (2.9) and parameter values in Table 2.1, more than 60% of the demand should be served within 7 min. Figure 2.12 indicates that when the average demand quantity model that does not consider the stochasticity of demand is used for location selection, the percentage of demand that can be served within 7 min is below 60% throughout the year. In contrast, when the spatial stochasticity of demand is considered, the service level is significantly improved to more than 60%

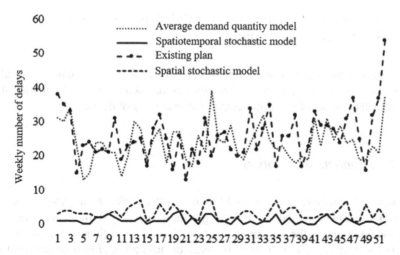

Fig. 2.11 Comparison of weekly times of delay

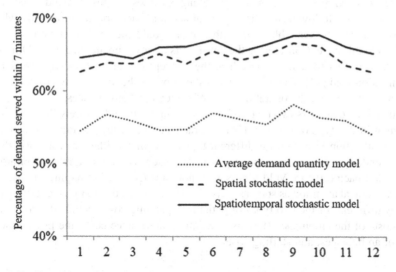

Fig. 2.12 Comparison of percentages at which demand is met within 7 min

throughout the year. If the spatiotemporal stochastic model is used, the service level can be enhanced further.

It should be noted that the above models and calculations assume there are always sufficient ambulances at each station, which inevitably overestimates the plan's performance. In the next section, the model will consider the number of ambulances to be allocated in each station.

2.3 Allocation of Ambulance Considering Spatiotemporal Stochasticity of Demand

This section considers both the location selection for ambulance stations and allocating the appropriate number of ambulances to each station. The model also considers the impact of the spatiotemporal stochasticity of demand.

2.3.1 Problem Description

Maintaining generality, assume an EMS network contains K demand zones and M candidate ambulance stations. Referring to the research by Borrás and Pastor [13], the model introduces the concept of the busy fraction of stations to indicate that a station's service capacity is limited. For each demand zone, H stations are required for providing services to the zone, including one primary station of first-tier priority and $H-1$ standby stations. When providing services to this demand zone, the standby stations follow a strict arrangement about service prioritisation: only when no ambulances are available at the hth station would the $(h+1)$th station provide services to this zone. Considering the constraints of government budgets and limited resources, in this model, we introduce the concept of the total social cost as the optimisation goal [14]. The total social cost comprises the loss cost due to delays of patient treatment and the operating costs of stations and ambulances.

The model considers two types of patients—mildly ill and severely ill—which is common in this type of research [14]. In practice, emergency departments also use this classification to categorise different types of demand. Illnesses categorised as severe endanger life or have poor prognoses, such as cardiac arrest, respiratory arrest, and haemorrhage. Mild illnesses do not endanger life but require the patient to seek medical attention as soon as possible. The loss cost due to treatment delays is clearly different for the two types of patients. Operating costs include the construction costs of the ambulance stations, the daily maintenance costs, the procurement cost of ambulances, and staffing costs.

2.3.2 Model Construction

Explanations of symbols:

α_{ijh}: 0–1 decision variable—if station j is a candidate station for serving demand zone i with the hth service prioritisation $\alpha_{ijh} = 1$; otherwise $\alpha_{ijh} = 0$

x_j: decision variable, the number of ambulances allocated to station j

y_j: 0–1 variable—if station j is used, $y_j = 1$; otherwise $y_j = 0$

Z: the total number of days in the planning period; if the planning period is a year, the value is 365

C_{Ti}: the expected loss cost in demand zone i caused by patient treatment delays

C_S: the average annual operating cost of each station

C_A: the average annual operating cost of each ambulance

t_{ij}: a random variable, the driving time from station j to demand zone i, with an average value of $\overline{t_{ij}}$

T_{wait}: the average waiting time when there is no ambulance available in the system

Ts_h: the driving time from the hth prioritised station to the demand zone should be less than Ts_h

D_i: a random variable, the total daily EMS demand of zone i, and $D_i \sim N(d_{\mu i}, d_{\sigma i})$

C_{rp}: expected loss cost due to delays in treating mildly ill patients; it is a function of t_{ij}

C_{sp}: expected loss cost due to delays in treating severely ill patients; it is a function of t_{ij}

w_r: the loss cost per unit of time caused by delays in treating mildly ill patients

w_s: the loss cost per unit of time caused by delays in treating severely ill patients

P_s: percentage of severely ill patients in total patients

q: busy ratio of each station

Φ: the proportion of demand that needs to be served by the first-tier priority station within time t^*, where t^* is an ideal service time required by government

λ_j: the average daily demand quantity that is served by station j

μ_b: the ambulance service rate (the demand quantity served by an ambulance in an hour)

A: the maximum number of ambulances that are available for allocation in the EMS system

η: a very large positive number

The objective function is to minimise the total social cost:

$$\min f = \sum_j y_j \cdot C_s + \sum_j x_j \cdot C_A + \sum_i C_{Ti} \tag{2.26}$$

The model needs to satisfy the following constraints:

$$C_{Ti} = Z \cdot d_{\mu i} \cdot \left(P_s \cdot C_{sp}(t_{ij}) + (1 - P_s) \cdot C_{rp}(t_{ij})\right) \tag{2.27}$$

$$C_{sp}(t_{ij}) = w_s \cdot \left[\sum_h \sum_j \alpha_{ijh} \cdot q^{h-1} \cdot (1 - q) \cdot \left(E(t_{ij}|t_{ij} > T_{S1}) - T_{S1}\right) \cdot \Pr(t_{ij} > T_{S1})\right.$$

$$\left. + q^H(T_{wait} - T_{S1})\right], \quad \forall i \in \{1, 2, \ldots, K\} \tag{2.28}$$

$$C_{rp}(t_{ij}) = w_r \cdot \left[\sum_h \sum_j \alpha_{ijh} \cdot q^{h-1} \cdot (1-q) \cdot \left(E(t_{ij}|t_{ij} > T_{S1}) - T_{S1} \right) \cdot \Pr(t_{ij} > T_{S1}) \right.$$
$$\left. + q^H (T_{wait} - T_{S1}) \right], \quad \forall i \in \{1, 2, \ldots, K\} \tag{2.29}$$

$$\sum_i D_i \cdot \sum_j \Pr(t_{ij} \le t^*) \cdot \alpha_{ij1} \ge \phi \cdot \sum_i D_i, \tag{2.30}$$

$$\sum_j t_{ij} \alpha_{ijh} \le T_{Sh}, \quad \forall i \in \{1, 2, \ldots, K\}, \forall h \in \{1, 2, \ldots, H\} \tag{2.31}$$

$$\lambda_j = \sum_i d_{\mu i} \left(\sum_h q^{h-1} (1-q) \alpha_{ij}^h \right), \quad \forall j \in \{1, 2, \ldots, M\} \tag{2.32}$$

$$\lambda/24 \le q \mu_b x_j, \quad \forall j \in \{1, 2, \ldots, M\} \tag{2.33}$$

$$\sum_j x_j \le A, \tag{2.34}$$

$$\sum_j \alpha_{ijh} = 1, \quad \forall i \in \{1, 2, \ldots, K\}, \forall h \in \{1, 2, \ldots, H\} \tag{2.35}$$

$$\sum_h \alpha_{ijh} = 1, \quad \forall i \in \{1, 2, \ldots, K\}, \forall j \in \{1, 2, \ldots, M\} \tag{2.36}$$

$$y_j \ge \frac{\sum_i \alpha_{ijh}}{\eta}, \quad \forall j \in \{1, 2, \ldots, M\}, \forall h \in \{1, 2, \ldots, H\} \tag{2.37}$$

$$y_j \le \sum_h \sum_i \alpha_{ijh}, \quad \forall j \in \{1, 2, \ldots, M\} \tag{2.38}$$

$$x_j \le \eta \cdot y_j, \quad \forall j \in \{1, 2, \ldots, M\} \tag{2.39}$$

$$x_j \ge y_j, \quad \forall j \in \{1, 2, \ldots, M\} \tag{2.40}$$

Formula (2.27) denotes the expected loss cost in demand zone i caused by patient treatment delays, including the costs due to delays in treating both mildly ill and severely ill patients. In providing services, the government makes a commitment to the public that under normal situations, an ambulance will reach the demand point within the time of T_{S1}, and T_{S1} determines the coverage radius of the first-tier station. If the ambulance does not meet this standard, there will be a punitive cost, which may result from a worsening of the patient's condition due to treatment delay or from the patient's dissatisfaction with the time delay of the EMS. Formulas (2.28) and (2.29) calculate the loss cost for severely ill and mildly ill patients, respectively. In formula (2.28), the expected time delay of a demand zone needs to be calculated based on stations' busy ratio q. $E(t_{ij}| t_{ij} > T_{s1})$ indicates that when the driving time from station j to demand zone i is greater than time T_{S1}, the expected service time delay for station j is calculated by subtracting T_{S1} from the expected driving time from station j to zone i. Constraint (2.30) requires that φ percent of the demand can be served by the primary station within time t^*, where $\Pr(t_{ij} \leq t^*)$ denotes the probability that the driving time from station j to demand zone i is less than a certain standard time t^*. Constraint (2.31) requires that the driving time from the hth prioritised station of demand zone i to the zone should not exceed T_{Sh}. This constraint is similar to the coverage radiuses in other studies. Formula (2.32) calculates the expected demand quantity that station j will be required to serve. Constraint (2.33) requires that the service capacity allocated to station j should be able to meet the expected demand calculated in formula (2.32). Constraint (2.34) is a resource constraint, indicating that the total number of ambulances in the EMS system cannot exceed A. Constraint (2.35) ensures that for each demand zone i, there is only one hth prioritised station. Constraint (2.36) ensures that for each demand zone, the priority level of station j is unique; in other words, station j cannot be a first-tier priority station while also a second-tier priority station for zone i. Constraints (2.37) and (2.38) respectively ensure that when station j is used, $y_j = 1$, and when it is not used, $y_j = 0$, where η is a very large positive number. Similarly, constraints (2.39) and (2.40) ensure that when station j is used, there are ambulances allocated for the station, namely, $x_j > 0$, otherwise $x_j = 0$.

Constraints (2.30) and (2.31) in the above model contain random variables, including the demand quantity D_i generated in the demand zone and driving time t_{ij}. Similar to the treatment in the previous section, the research employs the chance-constrained programming method to solve the model.

2.3.3 Case Analysis and Discussion

The EMS service data in Songjiang District, Shanghai, is used to test the effectiveness of the model. The setting of standby stations is the same as in Sect. 2.2, and there are 15 stations in the case study.

The value assignments for the model's parameters are shown in Table 2.4. Assume each demand point is served by one primary station and two standby stations, namely, $H = 3$. The cost to construct an ambulance station is approximately 1,500,000 RMB, and the ambulance station can be used for 30 years. The average operating cost of a station is approximately 200,000 RMB per year. Therefore, $C_S = 1,500,000$ RMB/30 + 200,000 = 250,000 RMB. Each ambulance costs approximately 450,000 RMB and has a 15-year useful life. A driver, stretcher carrier and doctor are assigned to each ambulance, and their average monthly salary is 5000 RMB. The costs of fuel and maintenance of each ambulance are approximately 60,000 RMB per year. Therefore, $C_A = 450,000$ RMB/15 + 5000 RMB × 3 × 12 + 60,000 RMB = 270,000 RMB. The percentage of

Table 2.4 Value assignments for parameters of the ambulance allocation model

Parameter	Value
K	30
M	15
H	3
CS	250,000 RMB
CA	270,000 RMB
Ps	0.07662
w_s	10,000 RMB
w_r	500 RMB
t^*	7 min
Ts_1	12 min
Ts_2	15 min
Ts_3	20 min
T_{wait}	22 min
φ	0.6
A	40
μ	0.68
q	0.3
θ_1	0.1
θ_2	0.1
θ_3	0.1

severely ill patients P_s is derived from historical EMS data in Shanghai. The loss costs per unit of time caused by delays in treating mildly ill and severely ill patients, w_s and dw_r, respectively, are determined through consulting managers at emergency departments and are also based on cases in which EMS delays have resulted in loss of lives and required economic compensation. The value assignment for this parameter can also be substantiated by [14]. The value assignments for t^* and T_{Sh} draw from generally adopted radiuses for coverage standards in existing coverage models [12]. The value assignments for φ and A are mainly based on the current conditions of medical infrastructure and health services in Shanghai. The EMS centre hopes that 60% of the demand can be served within 7 min; if the response time exceeds 12 min, a delay is considered to have occurred. The time delay is the total response time minus T_{S1}. Given the constraints of government budget and staffing, the total number of ambulances in the planning area cannot exceed 40. However, in performing the sensitivity analysis for the stations' busy ratio q, this study appropriately relaxes this constraint to a certain extent. The ambulance service rate is derived from Songjiang District's EMS statistics for 2013–2014. The stations' busy ratio q is temporarily set at 0.3. In most research, q is set within a range between 0.1 and 0.6 [15]. Later in this study, a set of different values are assigned to q to test its impact on the system's performance and optimal solution.

The optimal plan generated by the ambulance allocation model that considers the spatiotemporal stochasticity of demand is presented in Table 2.5, and the distribution of used stations under this plan is shown in Fig. 2.13. The new optimal plan will

Table 2.5 Ambulance allocation plan generated by the spatiotemporal model

| | No. of ambulances | Number of stations | Ambulance allocation plan for candidate stations | | | | | | | | | | | | | | |
			1	2	3	4	5	6	7	8	9	10	11	12	13	14	15
Spatiotemporal model	19	13	2	2	3	1	2	1	1	2	1	1	1	0	1	0	1
Existing plan	26	8	5	2	3	3	3	2	4	4	0	0	0	0	0	0	0

Fig. 2.13 Station locations under the ambulance allocation model

Table 2.6 Performance of ambulance allocation plan derived from the spatiotemporal model

	Total cost (Cplex forecast)	Total cost (based on real data)	Average response time	Time delay	Number of delays
Spatiotemporal model	9,664,363	9,160,349	6.86 min	635.52 min	173
Existing plan	–	13,660,245	10.73 min	3779.88 min	1352

require 13 ambulance stations, 5 more than in the existing plan. A total of 19 ambulances need to be allocated, 7 ambulances less than in the existing plan.

The performance of the plan derived from the ambulance allocation model is shown in Table 2.6, in which, the total cost (Cplex forecasted) is the plan's optimal cost through theoretical calculations based on the assumptions of the spatial distribution of demand. The cost based on real data is the total cost calculated using the real data from Songjiang District (including the time and location of demand occurrences). This verification allows us to test the effectiveness of the model's optimal plan. Table 2.6 indicates that although the spatiotemporal model proposed in this study requires more stations, it reduces the number of ambulances and significantly reduces the time delays and number of delays. Under the optimised new plan, the total cost is 33% less than that of the existing ambulance allocation plan in the Songjiang District.

References

1. R. McCormack, G. Coates, A simulation model to enable the optimization of ambulance fleet allocation and base station location for increased patient survival. Eur. J. Oper. Res. **247**(1), 294–309 (2015)
2. G. McLachlan, D. Peel, *Finite Mixture Models* (Wiley, 2004)
3. R.L. Streit, *Poisson Point Processes: Imaging Tracking and Sensing* (Springer, Boston, MA, 2010)
4. T.M. Nguyen, Q.J. Wu, Fast and robust spatially constrained Gaussian mixture model for image segmentation. IEEE Trans Circ. Syst. Vid. Technol. **23**(4), 621–635 (2013)
5. G. Gallego, G. Van Ryzin, Optimal dynamic pricing of inventories with stochastic demand over finite horizons. Manag. Sci. **40**(8), 999–1020 (1994)
6. M. Ng, Distribution-free vessel deployment for liner shipping. Eur. J. Oper. Res. **238**(3), 858–862 (2014)
7. V. Bélanger, Y. Kergosien, A. Ruiz, P. Soriano, An empirical comparison of relocation strategies in real-time ambulance fleet management. Comput. Ind. Eng. **94**, 216–229 (2016)
8. S.S.W. Lam, C.B.L. Ng, F.N.H.L. Nguyen, Y.Y. Ng, M.E.H. Ong, Simulation-based decision support framework for dynamic ambulance redeployment in Singapore. Int. J. Med. Inform. **106**, 37–47 (2017)
9. K. Schneeberger, K.F. Doerner, A. Kurz, M. Schilde, Ambulance location and relocation models in a crisis. CEJOR **24**(1), 1–27 (2016)
10. S. Fang, W. Xing, *Linear Conic Optimization* (Sciences Press, Beijing, 2013)
11. W.Y. Chiu, B.S. Chen, Mobile location estimation in urban areas using mixed Manhattan/ Euclidean norm and convex optimization. IEEE Trans. Wirel. Commun. **8**(1), 414–423 (2009)
12. M. Gendreau, G. Laporte, F. Semet, Solving an ambulance location model by tabu search. Locat. Sci. **5**(2), 75–88 (1997)
13. F. Borrás, J.T. Pastor, The ex-post evaluation of the minimum local reliability level: an enhanced probabilistic location set covering model. Ann. Oper. Res. **111**(1), 51–74 (2002)
14. Q. Su, Q.Y. Luo, S.H. Huang, Cost-effective analyses for emergency medical services deployment: a case study in Shanghai. Int. J. Prod. Econ. **163**, 112–123 (2015)
15. A. Shariat-Mohaymany, M. Babaei, S. Moadi, S.M. Amiripour, Linear upper-bound unavailability set covering models for locating ambulances: application to Tehran rural roads. Eur. J. Oper. Res. **221**(1), 263–272 (2012)

Chapter 3
Improving Diagnostic Accuracy Based on Multiple Cutoff Levels of Multiple Tumour Markers

Artificial intelligence (AI) and data mining (DM) can play important roles in medical services. The disease diagnostic accuracy can be improved through the analysis of massive historical data, and an optimal treatment plan can be derived by analysing medical service process data. In this chapter, a new developed diagnostic algorithm of tumour markers to colorectal cancer is used as an example to demonstrate how AI and DM can be employed to improve the diagnostic value of tumour markers.

3.1 Colorectal Cancer and Its Diagnostic Methods

3.1.1 Diagnosis of Colorectal Cancer

Colorectal cancer is a common malignancy that ranks second in Western countries in terms of mortality among all tumours and fourth in China in terms of incidence among all cancers. Traditionally, the most widely used screening methods for colorectal cancer are colonoscopy and the faecal occult blood (FOB) test. Clinical trials have shown that the application of colonoscopy can effectively reduce mortality from colorectal cancer. However, colonoscopy has limited application because of the high cost and intolerance in some patients. Meanwhile, the FOB test has low specificity and sensitivity.

In recent years, the application value of an increasing number of tumour markers has been demonstrated for the screening and auxiliary diagnosis of colorectal cancer. A large number of studies have focused on determining the cutoff level for tumour markers to distinguish between normal and abnormal situations and therefore improve diagnosis accuracy [1–4]. Usually, there is only one cutoff point for each tumour marker. This single cutoff point tumour marker-based diagnosis method is simple to use but is associated with two problems. First, the detection value of a tumour marker can spread broadly, say from 0 to 550. For instance, if the cutoff value is set to 5, the patient will be judged as negative if the test result is <5, and the

Q. Su, *Healthcare Operations Management*, SpringerBriefs in Service Science,
https://doi.org/10.1007/978-3-031-13397-8_3

patient will be judged as positive if the test result is a value from 5 to 550. One can see that single cutoff point is too imprecise to induce information loss on the detection results. Second, this diagnostic approach considers each tumour marker independently. When multiple tumour markers are jointly applied in the disease diagnosis. It is impossible to consider the combined diagnostic effect of multiple tumour markers.

Consequently, we propose a novel diagnostic approach that can calculate out multiple cutoff levels for each tumour marker based on the applications of the genetic algorithm (GA) and rough set theory. In this, the rough set-based rules extracting technology is utilised, and the GA algorithm with the best sensitivity and specificity value as the objective function is applied, thereby the optimal multiple cutoff levels for tumour markers can be calculated accordingly. In addition, orthogonal experiment technology is used to enhance diagnostic accuracy further. Finally, a set of real diagnostic data for colorectal cancer are used to verify the effectiveness of the proposed method in improving the diagnostic accuracy for colorectal cancer.

3.1.2   Indexes and Accuracy of Diagnosis

The basic medical indexes commonly used in medical diagnosis include the sensitivity (Se), specificity (Sp), and receiver operating characteristic (ROC) curve. In which, Se denotes the probability that a patient with a disease is correctly diagnosed, i.e., the true positive rate; 1-Se corresponds to the probability that a patient is erroneously diagnosed as healthy, i.e., the false-negative rate. Sp denotes the probability that a healthy individual is correctly diagnosed as healthy, i.e., the true negative rate; 1-Sp denotes the probability that a healthy individual is erroneously diagnosed as a patient with disease, i.e., the false-positive rate. There is a tradeoff relationship between Se and Sp.

The Encyclopedia of Biostatistics defines the ROC as "a quantitative method for determining how well experimental subjects, professional diagnosticians, and prognosticators perform when they are required to make a series of judgments or decisions." The ROC curve is plotted using the false positive rate (1-Sp) as the abscissa and the true positive rate (Se) as the ordinate. Given a set of diagnostic data, each possible cutoff value corresponds to a pair of Se and Sp values, that is, the coordinates of a point. The ROC curve is generated by connecting all points corresponding to different cutoff levels with a smooth curve, as shown in Fig. 3.1.

Generally speaking, the area under the ROC curve (AUC) is an internationally recognised objective criterion for diagnostic accuracy. Therefore, the AUC can be used to compare the performance of different detection approaches (tumour markers) in terms of diagnostic accuracy. The suitable cutoff level for a detection approach can be selected from the ROC curve based on the Se and Sp values that doctors wish to achieve. For example, if doctors want to maximise the Sp with no restrictions on Se, c_1 in Fig. 3.1 should be selected as the cutoff level. As the values of Se and Sp

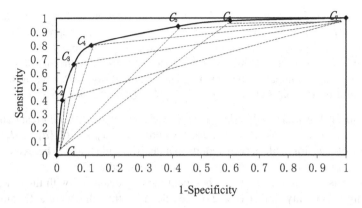

Fig. 3.1 The ROC curve for a diagnostic scheme

should be determined based on the disease type, incidence, and diagnosis cost, the selection of appropriate Se and Sp levels may change with basic conditions and is, therefore, debatable [5]. In practice, the most commonly used method is to select the cutoff level with the best overall Se and Sp, as shown in the upper left corner of the ROC curve in Fig. 3.1. Quantitatively, this cutoff level corresponds to the largest area under the dashed line, which can be calculated using Eq. (3.1). This criterion was used in our study to select the optimal multiple cutoff levels.

$$\text{Area} = 1 - \left[\frac{\text{Se} \times (1 - \text{Sp})}{2} + \frac{\text{Sp} \times (1 - \text{Se})}{2} + (1 - \text{Se}) \times (1 - \text{Sp}) \right]$$
$$= \frac{\text{Se} + \text{Sp}}{2} \tag{3.1}$$

3.2 Algorithm for Setting Multiple Cutoff Levels Based on GA and Rough Set Theory

3.2.1 Basic Concept of the Rough Set

Pawlak proposed rough set theory in 1982 [6]. The rough set theory can be used to describe incomplete, imprecise and inconsistent information so as to reveal hidden knowledge and potential patterns. To facilitate the application of rough set theory in this research, some basic concepts are introduced as follows.

Definition 1: A quadruple $S = \langle U, A, V, f \rangle$ is an information system. In which, $U = \{x_1, x_2, \cdots, x_n\}$ represents the discourse domain set consists of a finite number of objects. $A = C \cup D$ represents the set of a finite number of attributes, where C is the condition attribute set and D is the decision attribute set (representing the categories to which objects belong), with $C \cap D = \varnothing$. Information systems with decision attributes can be represented by a decision table. $V = U_{a \in A} V_a$ represents the set of attribute values, where V_a represents the value range of attribute a. $f : U \times A \to V$ is an information function that assigns an attribute value to each attribute of an object.

Objects with identical values in a given set of attribute P have a so-called indiscernibility relation: $\text{IND}(P) = \{(x_i, x_j) \in U \times U | \forall a \in P, f(x_i, a) = f(x_j, a)\}$.

Definition 2: For a given decision table S, each object $x(x \in U)$ corresponds to a sequence, $c_1(x), \ldots, c_m(x), d_1(x), \cdots, d_n(x)$, where $\{c_1, \ldots c_m\} = C$, $\{d_1, \ldots d_n\} = D$. Each row of decision table S corresponds to a decision rule that can be expressed as $c_1(x), \ldots, c_m(x) \to d_1(x), \cdots, d_n(x)$, which is abbreviated as $C_x \to D_x$.

Each decision rule $C_x \to D_x$ can be quantitatively evaluated with three indexes, i.e., strength, certainty, and coverage of the rule. The strength (str) of a decision rule $C_x \to D_x$ is evaluated by $\text{str}_x(C, D) = \frac{|C(x) \cap D(x)|}{|U|}$. The certainty (cer) of the decision rule $C_x \to D_x$ is given by $\text{cer}_x(C, D) = \frac{|C(x) \cap D(x)|}{|C(x)|}$. The coverage (cov) of the decision rule $C_x \to D_x$ is given by $\text{cov}_x(C, D) = \frac{|C(x) \cap D(x)|}{|D(x)|}$. In which, $|X|$ denotes the cardinality of the set X.

3.2.2 Rough Set Theory-Based Diagnostic Accuracy Evaluation

The problem of colorectal cancer diagnosis with multiple tumour markers can be viewed as distinguishing between a healthy individual D_1 and a colorectal cancer patient D_2 based on detection results obtained using multiple tumour markers. The detection and diagnostic results extracted from medical records form a decision table S to be analysed. Due to the complexity of patients' conditions, tumour markers with the same value can correspond to different final diagnostic result, i.e., indiscernibility, as described by the rough set.

Rough set theory enables rules to be extracted from information table. Among many available algorithms for rule extraction, the attribute reduction algorithm was adopted in this study [7]. This algorithm can remove redundant and repetitive information and thus effectively extract all rules from the information table. The detailed steps of the attribute reduction algorithm are described as follows.

Step 1:

Evaluate the values of each attribute in the information table, record by record. The original value of the attribute is retained if conflicting records are found in the information table. If no conflicting records are found, delete the current attribute to form a new table. And if we can find records exactly the same as the current record in the new information table, the value of the current attribute in this record is labelled as "*." Otherwise, it is labelled as "?."

Step 2:

Label potential duplicate records as "#." (Note: the putative duplicate record must not be labelled as "*" or "?" for all condition attributes in order to avoid interfering with Step 3.)

Step 3:

Check each record labelled "?." If a decision can be made solely based on other attributes, except those labelled with "*" and "?," then change the label "?" to "*"; otherwise, modify the label "?" to the original attribute value. If all the condition attribute values of a record are labelled as "*" or "?," then change the attribute values labelled "?" to the original values.

Step 4:

Delete records with all condition attributes labelled as "*" and putative duplicate records.

Step 5:

If two records differ in only one condition attribute, which is labelled as "*" in one of the two records, and if we can determine the correct decision based on the value of the attribute labelled "*," then delete the other record; otherwise, delete the current record.

All the attribute values in the information table obtained using the aforementioned five-step reduction process are the value cores of the table, and all records are the rules of the information table.

The presence of indiscernibility may result in the certainty of decision rules being smaller than 1. According to the characteristics of attribute reduction and the detection indexes, data for a patient may meet two rules with different decision results simultaneously. In this case, the accuracy of each rule can be used as the probability for the final decision. The doctor can then inspect the probability of the diagnostic result and use the rule with accuracy >50% as the patient diagnosis. The rule-based diagnostic results of all patients are then compared with the actual results to calculate Se and Sp, from which *Area* is finally obtained according to Eq. (3.1).

3.2.3 Algorithm Design Based on the GA and Rough Set

The algorithm for evaluating diagnostic accuracy presented above is mainly based on rough set theory, where *Area* is used as an objective criterion to evaluate the effect of diagnostic decision-making. However, the rough set is a mathematical theory dealing with inaccurate, incomplete, and inconsistent knowledge that is suitable for processing discrete, not continuous, data. Both the methods for attribute reduction and diagnostic effect acquisition are based on the premise that the detection value of tumour markers are discrete. In practice, the detection of tumour markers generates continuous data with a wide range of values. Therefore, these continuous data must be discretised before the algorithm can be used.

The discretisation of continuous data has been extensively studied. A literature review reveals three methods for treating continuous attributes [8], namely, the concept tree, expert experience, and algorithm discretisation. As tumour marker data cannot be discretised using the concept tree, many studies have been conducted on setting a single cutoff level for tumour markers, which creates controversy among doctors. Based on their experience, it is impossible for doctors to discretise continuous data, which highlights the significance of research on setting of multiple cutoff levels.

Therefore, in this study, we developed a discretisation algorithm based on an integrated application of genetic algorithm (GA) and rough set. The design concept of the algorithm is as follows. First, multiple cutoff levels are set to segment the original continuous data into discrete data. Then, the diagnostic accuracy of different schemes for setting multiple cutoff levels is calculated by applying the method described in Sect. 3.2.2. Finally, the diagnostic accuracies for different schemes are compared, and the scheme with the highest accuracy is achieved as the optimal solution.

In this study, the GA designed for finding the optimal multiple cutoff levels of tumour markers is elaborated as follows.

1. Encoding Scheme

The encoding scheme should be determined first in the GA procedure. Since the detection values of tumour markers encompass a wide range, the commonly used binary encoding schemes would result in excessively difficult and long encoding. Considering the characteristics of the problem at hand, the real-valued encoding scheme is used to create the initial population. For example, setting two cutoff levels each for three tumour markers will result in a total of six cutoff levels for a chromosome (see Eq. 3.2). The cutoff levels are randomly generated within the value range of the tumour markers represented by FieldDR, as shown in Eq. (3.3). Combining Eqs. (3.2) and (3.3) yields the value range of the first tumour marker as [0, 550] with randomly generated cutoff levels of 3.42 and 5.78, the value range of the second tumour marker as [0, 500] with randomly generated cutoff levels of 30.45 and 90.77, and the value range of the third tumour marker as [0, 200] with randomly generated cutoff levels of 4.07 and 187.89. Setting the population number to 200, a total of 200 chromosomes.

$$Chr = [3.42 \; 5.78 \; 30.45 \; 90.77 \; 4.07 \; 187.89] \tag{3.2}$$

$$FieldDR = \begin{bmatrix} 0 & 0 & 0 & 0 & 0 & 0 \\ 550 & 550 & 500 & 500 & 200 & 200 \end{bmatrix} \tag{3.3}$$

2. The Fitness Function

The *Area* for different settings of multiple cutoff levels can be calculated using rough set theory according to Sect. 3.2.2 and used as the fitness function.

$$Chr_1 = [3.42 \; 5.78 \; \underline{30.45 \; 90.77 \; 4.07} \; 187.89] \rightarrow Chr_1' = [3.42 \; 5.78$$

$$\underline{18.98 \; 70.23 \; 80.93} \; 187.89\,]$$

$$Chr_2 = [9.28 \; 3.32 \; \underline{18.98 \; 70.23 \; 80.93} \; 12.88] \rightarrow Chr_2' = [9.28 \; 3.32$$

$$\underline{30.45 \; 90.77 \; 4.07} \; 12.88]$$

Fig. 3.2 Crossover operation of two chromosomes

3. Selection

Selection refers to the process by which chromosomes are selected from the current population to generate offspring according to the fitness function. In this study, the fitness proportionate selection method is utilised to produce the next generation (offspring) through roulette wheel selection.

Specifically, for a population of size m, $G = \{x_1, x_2, \ldots x_m\}$, the fitness of a chromosome $x_j \in G$ is $\text{Area}(x_j)$, and the probability that this chromosome is selected is $g_j = \dfrac{\text{Area}(x_j)}{\sum_{j=1}^{m} \text{Area}(x_j)}, j = 1, 2, \cdots m$.

4. Crossover

The crossover operation is performed on a number of selected chromosomes in the population according to a predetermined crossover probability P_c. For instance, chromosomes Chr_1 and Chr_2 are selected, a crossover interval is randomly generated, e.g., from gene 3 to gene 5; then, all the genes of the two chromosomes within this interval are exchanged to generate two new chromosomes Chr_1' and Chr_2', as shown in Fig. 3.2.

$$\begin{aligned} Chr_1 &= [3.42 \; 5.78 \; \underline{30.45 \; 90.77 \; 4.07} \; 187.89] \rightarrow Chr_1' \\ &= [3.42 \; 5.78 \; \underline{18.98 \; 70.23 \; 80.93} \; 187.89\,] \end{aligned}$$

$$\begin{aligned} Chr_2 &= [9.28 \; 3.32 \; \underline{18.98 \; 70.23 \; 80.93} \; 12.88] \rightarrow Chr_2' \\ &= [9.28 \; 3.32 \; \underline{30.45 \; 90.77 \; 4.07} \; 12.88] \end{aligned}$$

5. Mutation

The mutation operation is conducted on some chromosomes in the population according to a predetermined mutation probability P_m. For each mutation operation, an integer mp less than or equal to the length of the chromosome is generated randomly to indicate the gene $Gene(mp)$ that needs to be mutated. Then, the gene is changed to the value that is equal to the difference between the original value and the upper limit of the value range of the corresponding tumour marker, Max

$$Chr_3 = \begin{bmatrix} 7.32 & 67.38 & 20.19 & 190.47 & \underline{1.72} & 157.44 \end{bmatrix} \rightarrow Chr_3{}' =$$

$$\begin{bmatrix} 7.32 & 67.38 & 20.19 & 190.47 & \underline{198.28} & 157.44 \end{bmatrix}$$

$$FieldDR = \begin{bmatrix} 0 & 0 & 0 & 0 & 0 & 0 \\ 550 & 550 & 500 & 500 & \underline{200} & 200 \end{bmatrix}$$

Fig. 3.3 Mutation operation procedure

(FieldDR), as expressed in Eq. (3.4). Thus, new chromosomes are generated through mutation operations.

$$\text{Gene}(mp)' = \text{Max}(\text{FieldDR}) - \text{Gene}(mp) \qquad (3.4)$$

As an example, consider a chromosome Chr_3 with its fifth gene as the point of mutation. The value range of the corresponding tumour marker FieldDR has an upper limit of 200. Hence, based on Eq. (3.4), the value at the fifth gene is replaced with $200 - 1.72 = 198.28$. The mutation operation is illustrated in Fig. 3.3.

$$\begin{aligned} Chr_3 &= \begin{bmatrix} 7.32 & 67.38 & 20.19 & 190.47 & \underline{1.72} & 157.44 \end{bmatrix} \rightarrow Chr_3{}' \\ &= \begin{bmatrix} 7.32 & 67.38 & 20.19 & 190.47 & \underline{198.28} & 157.44 \end{bmatrix} \end{aligned}$$

$$FieldDR = \begin{bmatrix} 0 & 0 & 0 & 0 & 0 & 0 \\ 550 & 550 & 500 & 500 & \underline{200} & 200 \end{bmatrix}$$

6. Optimal Solution Retention Strategy

With the above five steps, the population will be generated and evolved to more and more outstanding offspring in terms of fitness function. However, the randomness of genetic operations (selection, crossover, and mutation) can result in the deterioration of chromosome with the highest fitness in the population, thereby adversely impacting the operation efficiency and convergence of the GA algorithm [9]. Therefore, an optimal chromosome retention strategy based on roulette selection is adopted, as detailed below.

Step 1: Find several chromosomes with the highest fitness in the current population. The selected chromosomes should not be identical to ensure diversity.

Step 2: Find several chromosomes with the lowest fitness in the current population. As the purpose of this strategy is to retain the optimal chromosome, the chromosomes with the lowest fitness can be identical.

Step 3: Replace the chromosomes with the lowest fitness in the current population with those with the highest fitness.

7. Algorithm Termination Condition

In the algorithm, through the abovementioned six steps, the population will be gradually evolved generation by generation. When the number of generation (Gen) reaches a predetermined maximum number of evolutionary generations (MAXGEN), the algorithm will be stopped and the chromosome with the largest AUC in the population will be taken as the optimal solution.

Figure 3.4 shows the flowchart for the algorithm for setting multiple cutoff levels. The GA chromosomes represent combinations of various cutoff levels that are used to discretise the continuous detection data of tumour markers. The rule set is then obtained from the discretised data by using the attribute reduction method of rough set theory. Thereafter, for each multiple cutoff levels scheme (chromosome), its *Area* can be calculated and used to evaluate its diagnosis accuracy. The evolution search capability of GA can result in a continuous increase in the diagnosis accuracy over generations. When the termination condition is met, the chromosome with the largest *Area* will be derived which corresponds to the optimal combination of multiple cutoff levels for tumour markers.

3.3 Application Example

3.3.1 Data Collection and Detection Methods

In this study, the detection results of three tumour markers (CEA, CA199, and CA50) were collected for patients who were hospitalised or physically examined from November 2004 to March 2008 in a hospital in Shanghai. Data for 124 cases (75 cancer patients and 49 healthy individuals) examined from November 2004 to November 2006 were used as the training data set, and data for 88 cases (47 cancer patients and 41 healthy individuals) examined from December 2006 to March 2008 were used as the testing data set.

Venous blood was collected from each patient, and the serum was separated by conventional centrifugation for testing. Blood samples were collected from patients in the colorectal cancer group 3 days before surgery. The CEA marker was detected through chemiluminescence analysis using a kit provided by DPC on an Immulite 1000 analyser (DPC, Tianjin, China) with a normal reference value of $<4.8\ \mu g/L$ and a detection value range of 0–$550\ \mu g/L$. The CA199 marker was detected using a kit from Roche on an Elecsys 2010 system (Roche, Germany) with a normal reference value of $<33\ U/mL$ and a detection value range of 0–$500\ U/mL$. The CA50 marker was detected using a kit provided by Xiehe Medical Technology Co., Ltd., on a multitube radioimmuno-γ counter (Model DFM-96, Zhongcheng Electromechanical Technology Development Co., Ltd, China) with a normal reference value of $<25\ U/mL$ and a detection value range of 0–$200\ U/mL$.

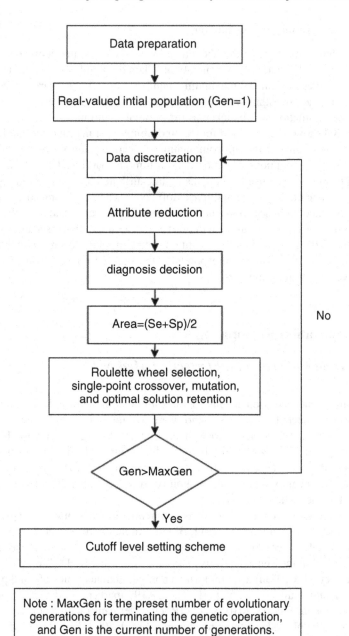

Fig. 3.4 Flowchart for the algorithm based on the GA and rough set theory for setting multiple cutoff levels

3.3.2 Algorithm Application Results

CEA is one of the most widely used tumour markers in clinical practice. However, only 50–70% of patients with colorectal cancer show an elevated CEA level, whereas CEA levels are also elevated in patients with other diseases (e.g., liver cirrhosis and ulcerative colitis) or malignant tumours with other sources. CA199 and CA50 are monoclonal antibodies derived from large intestine cancer that have also been widely used in colorectal cancer detection. As it is clinically very difficult to find a tumour marker with both high Se and Sp, two or more tumour markers are usually integrated and applied in cancer detection, which is called combined detection. Combined detection can be divided into serial and parallel experiments. A serial experiment is one in which abnormality is diagnosed if found in any of two or more experimental detection results, thereby improving the detection Se. A parallel experiment is one in which abnormality is diagnosed only if found in every detection result among two or more experimental detection results, thereby improving the detection Sp. It is obvious that regardless of whether the serial or parallel method is used, there is a tradeoff between Sp and Se, i.e., one is improved at the expense of the other. Therefore, the overall diagnostic performance is usually not considerably improved by the combined detection.

To verify the effectiveness of the proposed algorithm in improving diagnostic accuracy, the diagnostic results of serial and parallel experiments commonly used in clinical practice were compared in terms of Se and Sp, as well as the respective means (*Areas*), based on data of healthy individuals and colorectal cancer patients. The Se and Sp obtained by using the serial and parallel methods on the training data and testing data are shown In Tables 3.1 and 3.2, respectively.

Although the number of cutoff levels can be freely set for each tumour marker in the proposed algorithm, an excessive number of cutoff levels will reduce doctors' acceptance of the detection rules. Thus, the upper limit of the number of cutoff levels was set to three for each tumour marker in this study; i.e., the continuous data were

Table 3.1 Diagnostic results obtained using serial and parallel methods for the training set

Training data set		Combined detection	
		Serial method	Parallel method
Cancer group and healthy group	Sp	0.90	1
	Se	0.67	0.09
	Area	0.78	0.55

Table 3.2 Diagnostic results obtained using serial and parallel methods for the testing set

Testing data set		Combined experiment	
		Serial method	Parallel method
Cancer group and healthy group	Sp	0.90	1
	Se	0.65	0.15
	Area	0.77	0.58

discretised into four segments. In addition to comparing the performance of the proposed algorithm against those of serial/parallel experiments, the influence of combinations of different numbers of cutoff levels on diagnostic accuracy was investigated. As the three cutoff levels of three tumour markers can consist of a total of $3 \times 3 \times 3 = 27$ different combinations, the optimal combination is obtained through orthogonal experiments by which the experiment times can be reduced from 27 to 9 (Table 3.3). The cutoff levels corresponding to the nine cutoff level combinations in the orthogonal experiments are shown in Table 3.4. The results in Tables 3.3 and 3.4 were derived using the testing data set.

The statistical analysis of the orthogonal experiment results presented in Table 3.3 shows that the optimal cutoff level scheme is "3–3–2," in which, the highest value of *Area* is achieved. Therefore, the corresponding optimal values of multiple cutoff levels can be obtained from Table 3.4, i.e., 3.72, 150.26, 452.25 for CEA, 11.53, 17.56, 460.20 for CA199, and 14.06, 28.32 for CA50. These cutoff levels were used to discretise the training data set, based on which a diagnostic rule set was obtained through attribute reduction using rough set theory, as shown in Table 3.5. A total of 23 diagnostic rules were obtained from the training data set composed of data from 124 cases. The proposed algorithm uses attribute reduction to extract diagnostic rules rather than using str, cer, and cov to select rules. Consequently, a full set of rules was obtained, in which some rules are contradictory to each other (e.g., Rules 1 and 15). Such contradictions are commonly encountered during the actual diagnosis and treatment practices. Two patients (one is healthy and one has cancer) may have the same detection results; i.e., the two patients cannot be distinguished between based on existing detection indexes. Retaining contradictory rules effectively reflects objective facts. Despite a large number of rules, there is no overfitting, and the final diagnostic result is based on rules with higher certainty, whereby doctors can be informed of the accuracy of the diagnostic result. For example, the detection results for CEA, CA199, and CA50 of a patient were 3.2, 10.2, and 13, respectively. Based on the cutoff levels shown in Table 3.4, the data were discretised into 1, 1, and 1, which upon comparison with the rule sets were found to fit Rules 1 and 15 in Table 3.5. The accuracy of Rule 1 $(1,1,1 \rightarrow$ healthy) was 0.7381, and that of Rule 15 $(1,1,1 \rightarrow$ cancer) was 0.2619. Therefore, the result of Rule 1 was used as the diagnostic result for the patient; i.e., the patient was diagnosed as healthy.

Furthermore, the rules presented in Table 3.5 were used to evaluate the performance of the proposed algorithm on the testing data set, and the results are shown in Table 3.6.

Tables 3.1 and 3.2 show that the serial method significantly outperformed the parallel method. Therefore, the results of the serial method were used in the subsequent comparative analysis. A comparison of Tables 3.2 and 3.6 shows that the diagnostic accuracy (*Area*) is increased from 0.77 to 0.87.

Table 3.3 Comparison of the performances of serial/parallel experiments and the proposed algorithm

Test data		Cutoff level											
		Parallel experiment	Serial experiment	Algorithm 1-1-1	Algorithm 1-2-2	Algorithm 1-3-3	Algorithm 2-1-2	Algorithm 2-2-3	Algorithm 2-3-1	Algorithm 3-1-3	Algorithm 3-2-1	Algorithm 3-3-2
Healthy individuals vs. colorectal cancer patients	Sp	0.90	1	0.90	0.90	0.98	0.90	0.80	0.86	0.94	0.88	0.89
	Se	0.67	0.09	0.75	0.75	0.64	0.79	0.79	0.84	0.71	0.79	0.84
	Area	0.78	0.55	0.82	0.82	0.81	0.84	0.79	0.85	0.82	0.83	0.86

Note: "1-1-1" denotes that one cutoff level each was set for CEA, CA199, and CA50, and "3-3-2" denotes that 3, 3, and 2 cutoff levels were set for CEA, CA199, and CA50, respectively

Table 3.4 The values for the nine cutoff levels experiments

Cutoff-level scheme	CEA (0–550 µg/L)			CA199 (0–500 U/mL)			CA50 (0–200 U/mL)		
1-1-1	3.07			85.15			32.56		
1-2-2	3.07			4.53	85.15		32.72	47.02	
1-3-3	5.42			31.56	58.26	64.32	25.34	26.66	73.06
2-1-2	1.35	3.12		12.26			12.30	32.92	
2-2-3	5.46	504.66		11.28	27.48		13.95	28.58	80.22
2-3-1	3.07	7.09		11.25	16.10	445.74	13.56		
3-1-3	3.37	264.05	341.80	67.70			10.07	84.47	105.36
3-2-1	3.21	147.54	171.83	12.96	17.08		16.27		
3-3-2	3.72	150.26	452.25	11.53	17.56	460.20	14.06	28.32	

Table 3.5 Decision rule set obtained through attribute reduction

Number	CEA	CA 19-9	CA 50	Diagnosis	Strength	Certainty	Coverage
1	1	1	1	Healthy	0.25	0.7381	0.6327
2	1	2	2	Healthy	0.0242	1	0.0612
3	*	1	3	Healthy	0.0161	1	0.0408
4	1	3	1	Healthy	0.0484	1	0.1224
5	1	3	3	Healthy	0.0081	0.3333	0.0204
6	1	1	2	Healthy	0.0161	0.6667	0.0408
7	1	3	2	Healthy	0.0081	0.25	0.0204
8	2	1	1	Healthy	0.0081	0.0714	0.0204
9	1	2	1	Healthy	0.0081	0.1111	0.0204
10	2	2	1	Cancer	0.0081	0.0909	0.0204
11	2	3	*	Cancer	0.129	1	0.2133
12	1	3	3	Cancer	0.0161	0.6667	0.0267
13	1	2	1	Cancer	0.0645	0.8889	0.1067
14	*	4	*	Cancer	0.0161	1	0.0267
15	1	1	1	Cancer	0.0887	0.2619	0.1467
16	2	1	1	Cancer	0.1048	0.9286	0.1733
17	3	*	*	Cancer	0.0242	1	0.04
18	4	*	*	Cancer	0.0242	1	0.04
19	2	2	1	Cancer	0.0806	0.9091	0.1333
20	2	*	2	Cancer	0.0806	1	0.1333
21	1	3	2	Cancer	0.0242	0.75	0.04
22	*	2	3	Cancer	0.0081	1	0.0133
23	1	1	2	Cancer	0.0081	0.3333	0.0133

Note: '*' denotes any value

3.3.3   In-Depth Comparison Analysis

The results described above were based on the proposed algorithm, and the comparative analysis was based on the results of one-time calculation. The comparative

Table 3.6 Performance of proposed algorithm on the testing data set

		Cutoff levels
Testing data set		CEA (3.72, 150.26, 452.25) CA199 (11.53, 17.56, 460.20) CA50 (14.06, 28.32)
Cancer group and healthy group	Sp	0.87
	Se	0.86
	Area	0.87

analysis was subsequently extended to demonstrate the effectiveness of the proposed algorithm relative to that of other commonly used methods, such as intelligent algorithms and the medical serial algorithm, by using fivefold cross-validation. The statistical significance of the difference between the methods was explored using the t-test analysis.

The intelligent algorithms included the support vector machine (SVM), backpropagation neural network (BPNN), K-nearest neighbour (K-NN) method, and decision tree algorithm. To ensure the reliability and reproducibility of the results, we adopted standardised software packages or toolkits for these algorithms (LibSVM-2.89 for SVM, neural network toolbox 5.0 in MATLAB 7.2 for BPNN, the IBk algorithm in Weka 3.6 for K-NN, and the J48 algorithm in Weka 3.6 for decision tree). The "3–3–2" combination for the cutoff levels (Table 3.4) was again adopted for the proposed algorithm.

Table 3.7 is a comparison of the results obtained from applying fivefold cross-validation to each algorithm.

Tables 3.8 and 3.9 shows the results of a comparative analysis of the performance of the algorithms using the t-test analysis based on the results presented in Table 3.7. In Table 3.8, the null hypothesis is that the proposed method is inferior to the other algorithms, and the P value shows the hypothesis is invalid, with a confidence level in the range of 90–99%. Therefore, the results in Table 3.8 show that the proposed method outperforms other algorithms.

The null hypothesis in Table 3.9, except for the case of the decision tree method, is that the serial method is not significantly different from other algorithms. The P value shows that this hypothesis is valid. And the last row indicates that the serial method is significantly superior to the decision tree method with a confidence level of 95%.

In summary, the above analysis results disclose that the existing medical diagnostic method, i.e., the serial method, is more effective than the decision tree approach and has the same effect as SVM, BPNN, and KNN approaches. And all these approaches are inferior to the newly proposed method in this study.

Table 3.7 Comparison of the performances of various algorithms

		#1	#2	#3	#4	#5	Mean	Standard error
SVM[a]	Sp	0.8182	0.9375	0.8125	0.85	0.8824	0.8601	0.0515
	Se	0.7	0.7308	0.7692	0.7727	0.7778	0.7501	0.0336
	Area	0.7591	0.8341	0.7909	0.8114	0.8301	0.8051	0.0309
BPNN[b]	Sp	0.8182	0.846	0.8125	0.8	0.8824	0.8318	0.0329
	Se	0.75	0.75	0.6923	0.7727	0.7778	0.7486	0.0339
	Area	0.7841	0.798	0.7524	0.7864	0.8301	0.7902	0.0280
kNN[c]	Sp	0.8182	0.6875	0.625	0.8	0.7059	0.7273	0.0807
	Se	0.75	0.7307	0.8846	0.7273	0.9259	0.8037	0.0942
	Area	0.7841	0.7091	0.7548	0.7636	0.8159	0.7655	0.0393
Decision tree	Sp	0.9091	0.5625	0.5	0.85	0.7647	0.7173	0.1788
	Se	0.6	0.8077	0.8846	0.6818	0.7047	0.7358	0.1114
	Area	0.7546	0.6851	0.6923	0.7659	0.7347	0.7265	0.0364
Serial method	Sp	0.9545	1	0.875	0.8	0.8824	0.9024	0.0773
	Se	0.65	0.6538	0.6923	0.5909	0.7037	0.6581	0.0443
	Area	0.8023	0.8269	0.7837	0.6955	0.7931	0.7803	0.0501
Multiple-cutoff-level algorithm	Sp	0.7727	1	0.875	0.85	0.8235	0.8642	0.0848
	Se	0.85	0.8462	0.7308	0.8636	0.8889	0.8359	0.0611
	Area	0.8114	0.9231	0.8029	0.8568	0.8562	0.8501	0.0478

[a]The kernel function of the SVM was $K(x, y) = e^{-\gamma\|x-y\|^2}$, and the penalty factor C and kernel parameter γ were optimised using the internal commands of LibSVM-2.89
[b]The BPNN consisted of three layers, input, hidden, and output layers, with three, seven, and two nodes, respectively, and TANSIG and LOGSIG were used as the transfer functions of the hidden and output layers, respectively
[c]In each fold for the IBK algorithm, the parameter K was assigned a value from 1 to 10, and the optimal diagnostic performance was presented in the table

Table 3.8 Results of the t test for the difference between the performance of the proposed algorithm and that of other algorithms

Null hypothesis	P value
Multiple-cutoff-level algorithm $\leq$ SVM	0.0577
Multiple-cutoff-level algorithm $\leq$ BPNN	0.0210
Multiple-cutoff-level algorithm $\leq$ kNN	0.0078
Multiple-cutoff-level algorithm $\leq$ decision tree	0.0009
Multiple-cutoff-level algorithm $\leq$ serial method	0.0271

Table 3.9 Results of the *t* test for the difference between the performance of the serial method and that of other algorithms

Null hypothesis	P value
Serial method = SVM	0.3727
Serial method = BPNN	0.7088
Serial method = KNN	0.6184
Serial method $\leq$ decision tree	0.044

References

1. N.C. Armitage, A. Davidson, D. Tsikos, et al., A study of the reliability of carcinoembryonic antigen blood levels in following the course of colorectal cancer. Clin. Oncol. **10**, 141–147 (1984)
2. M.W. Wichmann, U. Lau-Werner, C. Muller, et al., Carcinoembryonic antigen for the detection of recurrent disease following curative resection of colorectal cancer. Anticancer Res. **20**, 4953–4955 (2000)
3. L.A. Carriquiry, A. Pineyro, Should carcinoembryonic antigen be used in the management of patients with colorectal cancer? Dis. Colon Rectum **42**, 921–9210 (1999)
4. H. Korner, K. Soreide, P.J. Stokkeland, et al., Diagnostic accuracy of serum carcinoembryonic antigen in recurrent colorectal cancer: a receiver operating characteristic curve analysis. Ann. Surg. Oncol. **14**(2), 417–423 (2006)
5. D.L. Streiner, J. Cairney, What's under the ROC? An introduction to receiver operating characteristic curves. Can. J. Psychiatr. **52**, 121–128 (2007)
6. Z. Pawlak, Rough sets. Int. J. Inf. Comput. Sci. **11**, 344–356 (1982)
7. L. Chang, G. Wang, Y. Wu, An approach to attribute reduction and rule generation based on rough set theory. J. Softw. **10**(11), 1206–1211 (1999)
8. D. Miao, A new method of discretization of continuous attributes in rough sets. Acta Automat. Sin. **27**(3), 297–302 (2001)
9. M. Zhou, S. Sun, *Genetic Algorithms: Theory and Applications* (National Defense Industry Press, Beijing, 1999)

Chapter 4
Robust Optimisation for Multiple Medical Service Project Scheduling Considering the Uncertainty of Activity Durations and Resource Allocation

In the field of medical service research, the scheduling of medical activities and resources has always been a difficult problem. Usually, a medical treatment process can handle multiple types of patients, and a series of care activities should be conducted for each patient with the assistance of different types of medical resources. Due to the strong instability of the medical service environment, the optimisation of the medical service process can be regarded as a multiple medical service project scheduling problem considering the uncertainty of activity durations and resource allocation.

To solve this problem, a multiple project robust optimisation scheduling model is established, in addition, an improved genetic algorithm (GA) is designed to computer out the optimal solution. The effectiveness of the model and algorithm is verified by solving the case of a medical service process in the orthopaedics department of the emergency centre in a hospital in Shanghai.

4.1 Introduction to the Multiple Project Scheduling and the Robust Optimisation

4.1.1 Multiple Project Scheduling

Research on project scheduling usually takes a single project as a research object to arrange execution times and allocate resources for activities. However, Turner found that more than 90% of enterprises are actually operating in a multiple project environment [1]. Multiple project scheduling refers to the simultaneous execution of multiple projects of varying sizes, activities, and progress that share a limited set of resources [2]. Compared with single project scheduling, multiple project scheduling research is more complex. Therefore, multiple project scheduling research is of great significance.

© The Author(s), under exclusive license to Springer Nature Switzerland AG 2022   63
Q. Su, *Healthcare Operations Management*, SpringerBriefs in Service Science,
https://doi.org/10.1007/978-3-031-13397-8_4

The conventional critical path method (CPM) and programme evaluation and review technique (PERT) are used to minimise project duration with an assumption of unlimited availability of resources for each project activity. Conversely, in real-life projects, resources are always limited, and it is difficult to satisfy the resource demand of concurrent activities [3]. In this circumstance, Kelley proposed the resource-constrained project scheduling problem (RCPSP) [4]. This problem has been proven to be NP hard. Increased problem scale and scarce resources make scheduling tasks more challenging and computationally complex. Recognition of these limitations has motivated researchers to develop different exact and heuristic solution procedures for solving resource-constrained project scheduling problems (RCPSPs) [3]. Taoa and Dongb considered alternative project structures when dealing with a multimode resource-constrained project scheduling problem [5]. And a hybrid metaheuristic algorithm was developed based on an AND-OR network to solve this NP-hard problem efficiently. To improve the calculation efficiency, an adapted tabu search algorithm and the non-dominated sorting genetic algorithm-II (NSGA-II) algorithm were jointly utilised.

Although there are few studies on multiple project scheduling, multiple project scheduling can be used in many daily life situations. For example, resource allocation involving the development of multiple new products [6] and even computing the resource allocation of internet servers can be considered multiple project scheduling [7]. Van Der Merwe indicates that the greatest difficulty of multiple project scheduling is the lack of control over all projects [8]. Due to the sharing of resources among multiple projects, the rational allocation of limited resources becomes the greatest challenge for multiple project scheduling [9]. Most of the common objective functions of multiple project scheduling problems aim to optimise the total completion time, but with the advancement of single project scheduling research, multiple project scheduling problems are further expanded. Some scholars have designed other objective functions, such as resource balance [10], and some have used more complex combinatorial objective functions [11] to describe a multiple project scheduling problem.

4.1.2 The Robust Optimisation

Because of the changing environment, the execution procedure of project is often unstable. In practice, project uncertainties are usually manifested in two aspects, i.e., the duration uncertainty and the resource demand uncertainty. In recent years, project management researches have been particularly concerned with project scheduling under uncertain scenarios. To this end, some robust optimisation methods are proposed. Robustness refers to the ability of a system to withstand the influence of uncertain factors. Robust optimisation has become one of the research hot topics in solving problems with uncertain scenarios.

Graves first proposed the concept of scheduling robustness [12]. Van de Vonder et al. took the robustness of the solution as the research objective and compared and tested a variety of heuristic programmes for project scheduling [13]. Bruni et al. constructed a robust joint probability constrained model to minimise the expected time of a project and used a phase decomposition algorithm to solve the problem [14]. Then, they established an adjustable robust optimisation model for a resource-constrained project scheduling problem with uncertain activity durations [15]. Additionally, they proposed two exact methods for a robust RCPSP under budgeted uncertainty, where a two-stage robust optimisation framework was used to address the inherent uncertainty in the activity durations [16].

Leus and Herrelen studied how to obtain robust resource allocation schemes [17]. Brčić et al. proposed the planning horizons-based proactive rescheduling for stochastic resource-constrained project scheduling problems [18]. Yamashita et al. constructed a minimal regret robust model and mean robust model with resource cost as the optimisation objective [19]. Xu and Xu studied the cross-enterprise project robust scheduling algorithm considering resource reliability [20]. Aritigues et al. designed a robust objective to minimise the absolute regret value of all scenarios for resource-constrained project scheduling problems and used a heuristic algorithm based on integer programming and scene relaxation to solve the earliest execution strategy of each activity [21].

4.2   Model Formulation

In this section, a multiple project scheduling model for medical services is constructed. The model needs to satisfy the following basic assumptions:

1. Each project is independent of the others.
2. Inside a project, the constraint relationship between activities is determined.
3. Each activity has only one mode of execution.
4. Consider the logical relationship of 0-delay; that is, as soon all the immediate preceding tasks are finished, the subsequent task will start immediately.
5. Only considers renewable resource constraints, and the types and numbers of renewable resources required by each activity are determined.
6. All projects share the same set of resources.

The basic symbols and the corresponding descriptions are listed in Table 4.1.

4.2.1   Multiple Objective Scheduling Model of Medical Service Projects

Like most project scheduling models, the general goal is to minimise the total completion time of the project. In this model, the first objective function is set as the shortest project delay time as follows:

Table 4.1 Symbols and their descriptions for the model

Symbol	Description
i	The serial number of medical projects, $i=1,2...,I$.
j	The serial number of medical activity. (i,j) indicates activity j in project i
t	The serial number of time, $t = 0,1,2....,T_f.$
T_f	T_f is the completion time of the last medical activity.
P_{ij}	The collection of activities subject to the immediately preceding activity (i,j)
d_{ij}	The duration of medical activity (i,j)
s_{ij}	The start time of medical activity (i,j)
k	The serial number of medical resources, $k = 1,2,...,m$ and m is the total number of renewable resources.
R_K	The total supply of resource k
r_{ijk}	The demand of resource k for medical activity (i,j)
A_t	The collection of medical activities carried out in t period.
f_{ij}	The finish time of medical activity j in project i
F_i	The finish time of medical project i.
D_i	The expected completion time of medical project i.
C_k	Unit time cost of renewable medical resource k.
E_k	Unit transfer cost of renewable medical resource k.

$$\min z_1 = \sum_{i}^{I} \max(0, F_i - D_i) \tag{4.1}$$

Here, a patient's medical treatment process is regarded as a medical service project. And a medical service project is different from a traditional engineering project. The critical resources in medical service projects are mainly human resources including doctors, nurses, and paramedics. In a department of hospital, all the patients will be served by the same group of professionals, thereafter, the professionals need to move among different projects and activities frequently. And this kind of frequently professional switching takes time and effort which can induce a huge waste of efficiency and cost. To control the waste, it is necessary to consider the balance and stability of resources in a medical service project. As a result, the demands of medical resources for different activities and projects will be more stable without frequent adjustments. According to [22], the stability of medical resources can be quantitatively measured by resource transfer/switching costs. Therefore, the second objective function of the scheduling model is as follows:

$$\min z_2 = \sum_{k=1}^{K} E_k \sum_{t=1}^{T_f} \left| \sum_{(i,\ j)\in A_t} r_{ijk} - \sum_{(i,\ j)\in A_{t-1}} r_{ijk} \right| \tag{4.2}$$

This equation represents the minimum total transfer cost of all the renewable medical resources within the total completion time of medical service projects, where E_k represents the unit transfer cost of renewable medical resource k.

In addition to considering the balance of resources, the supply of every renewable medical resource also needs to be considered. More specifically, we should consider the maximum number of resources that are available to the project within the execution period, that is, the level of resources. Accordingly, the third objective function is defined as follows:

$$\min z_3 = \sum_{k=1}^{K} C_k f[r_k(A_t)] \tag{4.3}$$

in which,

$$f[r_k(A_t)] = \max_{t=0,1,\dots,T_f} \left(\sum_{(i,\ j) \in A_t} r_{ijk} \right) \tag{4.4}$$

Formula 4.3 can be used to minimise the sum of the maximum cost of renewable medical resources for each time period, where C_k represents the unit time cost of renewable medical resource k. Formula 4.4 represents the maximum consumption level of medical resource k for time period t.

To comparatively evaluate the above three objectives, the following weighting procedures are used to unify the order of magnitude of the three objectives [23]:

$$z_\delta' = \frac{z_\delta}{z_\delta^{\max}} \tag{4.5}$$

Then, the comprehensive optimisation objective function for the multiple project scheduling model can be expressed as follows:

$$\min z = \eta_1 z_1' + \eta_2 z_2' + \eta_3 z_3' \tag{4.6}$$

S.t.

$$s_{ij} > s_{ih} + d_{ih} \ (i,\ h) \in p_{ij}, \forall i,j \tag{4.7}$$

$$\sum_{(i,\ j) \in A_t} r_{ijk} \le R_K \tag{4.8}$$

$$r_{ijk} \ge 0 \tag{4.9}$$

$$s_{ij} \ge 0 \tag{4.10}$$

in which, η_1, η_2, and η_3 represent the weights for the three optimisation objectives. Formulae 4.7–4.10 represent the constraints that need to be satisfied. Formula 4.7 indicates that each activity must be started after the completion of its predecessor activities, which is a logical constraint of an activity. Formula 4.8 indicates that the total amount of renewable medical resources required for a medical activity cannot exceed the supply of resources, which is the resource constraint of the activity. Formulae 4.9 and 4.10 ensure that the demand of renewable medical resources and the start time of each medical activity are nonnegative.

4.2.2 The Robust Optimisation Model of Medical Service Projects

For a certain type of patient, the diagnosis and treatment time for different patients may fluctuate remarkably due to the unique characteristics of patient and his/her special requirements. Therefore, it is necessary to consider the uncertainty of the activity duration in the medical service project scheduling.

To this end, a set of scenarios Π is introduced to depict different activity duration situations [24]. In this, $\Pi = \{1,2,3 \ldots ,\phi\}$ indicates that there are ϕ scenarios. Considering different scenarios, the abovementioned time-related parameters should be modified accordingly. Given the scenario φ, the duration of treatment activity (i, j) can be denoted as d_{ij}^{ϕ}. In Formula 4.1, the finish time of project i, F_i, should be changed to F_i^{φ}. In Formula 4.2, the completion time of the last treatment activity, T_f, should be changed to T_f^{φ}.

Then, a multiple objective robust optimisation scheduling model of multiple medical service projects can be established as follows:

$$\min \mathrm{MV} = M + \beta \sum_{\varphi \in \Pi} P_{\varphi} \left(M - z_{\varphi} \right)^2 \qquad (4.11)$$

S.t.

$$M = \sum_{\varphi \in \Pi} P_{\varphi} z_{\varphi} \qquad (4.12)$$

in which, P_{ϕ} denotes the probability of occurrence of the scenario φ; z_{φ} denotes the value of z under scenario φ, and β is the coefficient of variance.

4.3 Algorithm Design

With the continuous development of computer technology and the cross fusion of different academic fields, heuristic algorithms have been developed and utilised to solve project scheduling problems, such as genetic algorithms, simulated annealing algorithms, and tabu-search algorithms. In this work, referring to [25], a genetic algorithm is designed to search out the optimal solution for the multiple project scheduling problem. In each time of evolutionary calculation, a group of scheduling schemes are generated first which is called the evolution chromosomes or population. Then, the corresponding objective function values of the chromosomes are computed, by which, the duration of the multiple medical service projects and the demands of different medical resources can be calculated. Thereafter, the evolutionary operations, including crossover, mutation, and selection, are conducted on the chromosomes in population to produce the next generation of chromosomes. This procedure will go on and on until the optimal scheduling scheme with the shortest duration and the lowest resource demands is derived.

For robust optimisation, a scenario set Π corresponding to a number of samples are used to estimate robustness. As in [24], we select 50 cases as samples, each case includes three possible times, i.e., the most optimistic time, the most likely time, and the most pessimistic time. According to the data statistic based on the real medical cases, the probability of occurrence of these three times is set to 1/6, 2/3, and 1/6.

Given the above assumptions, the genetic algorithm for the multiple objective robust optimisation scheduling model is constructed as follows:

1. Coding Scheme of Chromosome

In this work, a random decimal encoding method is used to represent the execution priorities of activities in medical service projects. The chain of the randomly generated activity priority is regarded as a chromosome, and each activity of each project corresponds to a unique priority. For multiple simultaneously executing projects, a virtual activity is set in front of all projects as a starting activity. Then, with the AON network diagram of each project, a global storage adjacency matrix can be obtained, and the corresponding scheduling scheme can be generated by combining the random sequence of activity priorities [25]. Thereby, the resource demand level can be evaluated. When the resource demands are not satisfied, the earliest start time of an activity will be deferred by a unit of time. The resource demand evaluation and time deferring will be continuously iterating until the resource demands are satisfied. This procedure will be performed on all activities of all projects. Ultimately, the completion time of the latest activity will be regarded as the completion time of the multiple medical service projects.

2. Fitness Function

The fitness function designed for the multiple objective robust optimisation scheduling model is as follows:

$$f(x) = \frac{1}{M + \beta \sum_{\varphi \in \Pi} P_\varphi (M - z_\varphi)^2} \tag{4.13}$$

3. Selection Operation

In this work, roulette selection is adopted to select chromosome individuals for next generation. And the chromosomes with the superior fitness value will be kept in the next generation. The selection probability of each individual can be calculated as follows:

$$p(x) = \frac{f(x)}{\sum f(x)} \tag{4.14}$$

4. Crossover Operation

In this work, a two-point crossover operator is used. To avoid the overlapping of the activity priorities that may occur after crossover, the two-point crossover method proposed in [25] is employed. This method can generate the offspring that can inherit the genetic characteristics of the parent generation and ensure that the activity priority is unique.

5. Mutation Operation

Here, the central location variation method is adopted to perform mutation operation to avoid the occurrence of chromosome duplication.

The steps of the genetic algorithm are as follows:

Step 1: To determine the minimum supply of each renewable resource according to the actual situation.

Step 2: To generate 10 sets of random activity priorities as the initial population according to the encoding rules.

Step 3: The corresponding scheduling scheme is generated according to the activity priority. The target function value of the model is calculated according to the scheduling scheme and the supply of resources. Then the fitness function value of each individual is calculated accordingly.

Step 4: The individuals are selected according to the selection operation rule, and the crossover and mutation operations are performed to obtain the next generation of new activity priorities.

Step 5: To repeat steps 3 and 4 until to a certain predetermined iteration time and then go to the sixth step.

Step 6: To record the optimal scheduling scheme, the objective function value, and the current supply of each renewable resource.

Step 7: To adjust the supply of renewable resources according to the actual situation.

Step 8: To repeat steps 3, 4, 5, 6, and 7 until the demand for resources is satisfied.

Step 9: The objective function values are calculated and, thereby, the optimal resource allocation and scheduling scheme for multiple medical service projects are derived.

4.4 Case Analysis

In this section, the robust optimisation scheduling model is applied in practical multiple medical service projects to verify the effectiveness of the model and algorithm. The following examples and data are collected from the orthopaedic emergency trauma centre of a hospital in Shanghai. Patients in the orthopaedic emergency trauma centre are classified into three types as mild, moderate, or severe. The corresponding three types of medical treatment processes are regarded as three kinds of medical service projects designated as A, B, and C. The diagnosis and treatment activities of each type of patient are regarded as the activities of the medical service projects to be completed in hospital. Because each medical activity duration is uncertain and needs the assistance of medical resources, the multiple project robust optimisation model and its algorithm established in previous sections can be used to analyse the case, and the optimal scheduling scheme and resources allocation can be obtained. The network charts for the three types of projects are illustrated as follows:

The detailed explanations for the medical activities are listed as 'activity name' in Table 4.2.

4.4.1 Data Collection

The data for this case are derived based on field study and historical record analysis. Considering the uncertainty of the duration of medical activities, the most optimistic time, the most likely time, and the most pessimistic time are statistically calculated for each activity, as shown in Table 4.2.

According to the actual situation of a hospital, this work considers six renewable resources: doctor, nurse, paramedic, inspector, anaesthesiologist, and operating room. Table 4.3 shows the types and quantities of resources needed for each medical activity.

As listed in Table 4.4, to evaluate the resource allocation quantitatively, the unit time cost of each renewable resource is given. Considering the resource stability, the unit transfer cost of medical resources is also needed. Here, since an inspector generally does not involve location transfer, the unit transfer cost for inspector is 0. Additionally, the supply of each kind of medical resource in orthopaedics departments is limited, denoted as the maximum supply in Table 4.4.

Through on-the-spot investigation and interview with doctors and nurses in the hospital, the orthopaedics department of the emergency centre usually serves approximately 10–13 patients a day, most of whom are class A patients who do not need surgical treatment. The arrival of patients usually reaches a peak at 9 AM and 1 PM. As shown in Table 4.5, the 12 patients who were served by the department on 30 January 2018 are used as examples.

Table 4.2 Name and duration of the medical activities

Project type	Activity number	Activity name	Most optimistic duration (min)	Most likely duration (min)	Most pessimistic duration (min)
A	①	Emergency treatment	5	8	20
	②	Physical examination	5	10	20
	③	Regular test	40	70	120
	④	X-ray test	20	30	70
	⑤	CT test	40	60	100
	⑥	Diagnosis of the disease	10	40	80
B	①	Emergency treatment	5	8	20
	②	Medical history inquiry	5	8	15
	③	Early treatment	5	8	45
	④	Physical examination	5	10	20
	⑤	Urine test	20	40	100
	⑥	Debridement	20	35	45
	⑦	CT test	40	60	100
	⑧	Angiography	120	240	360
	⑨	X-ray test	20	30	70
	⑩	Specialist treatment	230	390	540
	⑪	Diagnosis of the disease	5	10	30
	⑫	Infectious disease detection	30	50	80
	⑬	Preoperative examination	60	80	120
	⑭	Special inspection 1	60	120	200
	⑮	Rating patient's condition	20	40	80
	⑯	Special inspection 2	10	30	60
	⑰	Prepare for surgery	60	120	240
	⑱	Surgery	60	120	360
C	①	Emergency treatment	5	8	15
	②	Medical history inquiry	5	8	15
	③	Early treatment	5	8	15

(continued)

Table 4.2 (continued)

Project type	Activity number	Activity name	Most optimistic duration (min)	Most likely duration (min)	Most pessimistic duration (min)
	④	Physical examination	5	8	15
	⑤	Blood test	60	80	120
	⑥	Diagnosis of the disease	15	30	45
	⑦	Special inspection 1	60	120	240
	⑧	Biochemical tests	60	80	240
	⑨	Urine test	20	40	100
	⑩	Special inspection 2	10	30	60
	⑪	Prepare for surgery	60	80	120
	⑫	Surgery	120	240	480

From the above table, the treatment process of the 12 patients is regarded as 12 medical service projects to be completed by the department. The arrival time of each patient is regarded as the beginning time of each project. Referring to Fig. 4.1, the network diagram of each project is determined according to the classification of the corresponding patient.

4.4.2 Determination of Relevant Parameters and Calculation of Scheduling Schemes

Referring to Formula 4.1, for the maximum value of Z_1, the study found that the maximum delay times for A, B, and C patients were 90, 695, and 350 min, respectively. Therefore, for this example, the maximum value of Z_1 is 1945 min. Referring to Formula 4.2, for the maximum value of Z_2, the number of resource transfers could not be estimated and could not be easily obtained by investigation. Thereafter, the maximum value of Z_2 is estimated using the genetic algorithm. When 200 iterations of GA calculation are finished, we can find the value of Z_2, which is 2250. Referring to Formula 4.3, the maximum value of Z_3 is the product of the maximum resource supply and its unit time cost, which is 29.66. Other parameter settings in the model are shown in Table 4.6.

The parameters of the genetic algorithm are as follows: the population size is 104, the initial population is 10, the crossover rate is 0.5, the mutation rate is 0.05, and the number of iterations is 200 generations.

Through the calculation, the following scheduling scheme is obtained: (A5,0), (A5,1), (A5,2), (A5,3), (A4,0), (A6,0), (A7,0), (A7,1), (A7,2), (A5,4), (A5,5),

Table 4.3 Required resources for the medical treatment activities

Project type	Activity number	Doctor	Nurse	Paramedic	Inspector	Anaesthesiologist	Operating room
A	①	1	1	0	0	0	0
	②	1	1	0	0	0	0
	③	0	0	0	1	0	0
	④	1	0	0	0	0	0
	⑤	1	0	0	0	0	0
	⑥	1	0	1	0	0	0
B	①	1	1	0	0	0	0
	②	1	1	1	0	0	0
	③	1	1	1	0	0	0
	④	1	1	1	1	0	0
	⑤	0	0	1	0	0	0
	⑥	1	1	1	0	0	0
	⑦	1	0	1	0	0	0
	⑧	1	0	1	0	0	0
	⑨	1	0	1	0	0	0
	⑩	1	1	1	1	0	0
	⑪	2	0	1	0	0	0
	⑫	2	0	0	1	0	0
	⑬	0	1	1	1	0	0
	⑭	0	1	1	1	0	0
	⑮	1	1	0	0	0	0
	⑯	0	0	1	1	0	0
	⑰	0	1	1	0	1	1
	⑱	1	1	0	0	0	1
C	①	2	2	2	0	0	0
	②	0	1	0	0	0	0

③	0	0	0	2	1	1
④	0	0	0	2	1	1
⑤	0	0	1	0	1	0
⑥	0	0	0	0	0	2
⑦	0	0	1	2	1	0
⑧	0	0	1	2	1	0
⑨	0	0	1	2	1	0
⑩	0	0	1	2	1	1
⑪	1	1	0	2	1	0
⑫	1	0	0	0	2	2

Table 4.4 Cost information and maximum supply of renewable resources

Name of resource	Cost of resource (¥)	Unit time cost (¥/min)	Unit transfer cost	Maximum supply
Doctor	18,000 (monthly salary)	1.25	40	4
Nurse	8000 (monthly salary)	0.56	20	5
Paramedic	5000 (monthly salary)	0.35	10	5
Inspector	10,000 (monthly salary)	0.69	0	5
Anaesthesiologist	10,000 (monthly salary)	0.69	30	2
Operating room	500 (hourly cost)	8.33	80	2

Table 4.5 Introduction of examples

ID	Sex	Patient condition	Date of medical treatment	Starting time for medical treatment	Classification of disease
A0	Female	Head trauma	2018-1-30	08:03:04	A
A1	Female	Fracture of ribs	2018-1-30	09:06:21	A
A2	Male	Head trauma	2018-1-30	09:12:31	A
A3	Male	Head trauma	2018-1-30	10:59:28	A
C	Female	Thoracic vertebra fracture	2018-1-30	12:51:56	C
A4	Male	Fracture of nasal bone	2018-1-30	13:06:38	A
A5	Female	Fracture of phalanx	2018-1-30	13:13:29	A
B	Male	Intertrochanteric fracture of femur	2018-1-30	14:20:13	B
A6	Male	Head trauma	2018-1-30	16:50:56	A
A7	Male	Head trauma	2018-1-30	17:34:43	A
A8	Male	Head trauma	2018-1-30	19:15:10	A
A9	Male	Head trauma	2018-1-30	22:09:12	A

(A5,6), (A7,3), (A0,0), (A0,1), (A0,2), (A0,4), (A0,5), (A3,0), (A3,1), (A3,2), (A3,3), (A3,4), (A3,5), (A3,6), (A6,1), (A6,2), (A6,3), (A6,4), (A6,5), (A6,6), (B,0), (B,1), (B,3), (B,2), (A0,3), (A0,6), (C,0), (C,1), (C,2), (C,3), (C,4), (C,5), (C,6), (C,7), (C,8), (C,10), (C,9), (C,11), (C,12), (A1,0), (A1,1), (A1,2), (A1,3), (A1,4), (A1,5), (A1,6), (A2,0), (A2,1), (A8,0), (A8,1), (A8,2), (A8,4), (A8,5), (A2,2), (A2,3), (A2,4), (A2,5), (A2,6), (A8,3), (A8,6), (B,4), (B,5), (B,6), (B,7), (B,8), (B,11), (B,9), (B,10), (B,12), (B,13), (B,15), (B,18), (B,14), (B,16), (A4,1), (A4,2), (A4,3), (A4,4), (A4,5), (A4,6), (B,17), (B,19), (B,20), (A7,4), (A7,5), (A7,6), (A9,0), (A9,1), (A9,2), (A9,3), (A9,4), (A9,5), (A9,6).

As shown in Table 4.7, the optimal supply of medical resources is derived.

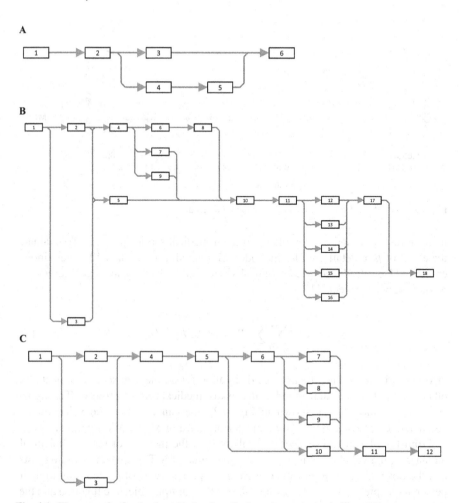

Fig. 4.1 The networks for the three kinds of medical service projects, A, B, and C

Table 4.6 The parameter value settings of the model

η_1	η_2	η_3	P_1	P_2	P_3	β
0.5	0.3	0.2	1/6	2/3	1/6	0.5

Table 4.7 Optimal supply of medical resources

Doctor	Nurse	Paramedic	Inspector	Anaesthesiologist	Operating room
4	3	3	4	1	1

4.4.3 Discussion on the Value of the Coefficient of Variance

One can see that, in Formula 4.11, the coefficient of variance β is critical for the optimisation calculation. So, it is important to explore the effect of β on the cost of

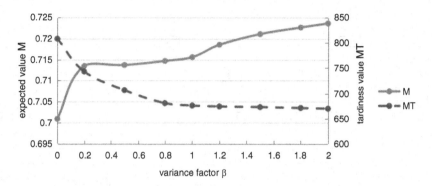

Fig. 4.2 The effect of the coefficient of variance β on M and MT

medical resources and the completion time of medical service projects. To evaluate the effect of β in detail, besides the index M defined in Formula 4.12, a new index entitled MT is introduced (see Formula 4.15) to analyse the total average tardiness of medical service projects [17].

$$\text{MT} = \sum_{\varphi \in \Pi} \sum_{i}^{I} P_{\varphi} \max (0, F_i - D_i) \qquad (4.15)$$

in which, MT represents the average delay time for all medical service projects. In other words, it can be understood as the risk of medical service projects. Through a series of calculations, as shown in Fig. 4.2, one can find that the value of the coefficient of variance β will affect the performance of M and MT significantly.

From Fig. 4.2, it can be seen that, along with the increase of the coefficient of variance β, the value of M increases and the value of MT decreases. This suggests that the hospital decision-makers can choose a proper value of β according to their personal risk preferences to the mean value of the multiple objective function and the delay time of medical service projects. Then, a corresponding optimal medical resource supply and the optimal scheduling scheme can be obtained accordingly.

As shown in Fig. 4.2, when the value of β varies from 0 to 0.2, the M value rises sharply, and the MT value decreases quickly. When the value of β is greater than 1, although the value of M is still rising gradually, the decline curve of the MT value has become gentle. Therefore, Fig. 4.2 can be used as a reference for decision-makers to determine the value of β.

References

1. J.R. Turner, *The Handbook of Project-Based Management* (McGraw Hill, New York, 2008)
2. S.E. Fricke, A.J. Shenhar, Managing multiple engineering projects in a manufacturing support environment. IEEE Trans. Eng. Manag. **47**(2), 258–268 (2000)

3. M.K. Ahsan, D. Tsao, Solving resource-constrained project scheduling problems with bi-criteria heuristic search techniques. J. Syst. Sci. Syst. Eng. **12**(2), 190–203 (2003)
4. J.E. Kelley, *The Critical Path Method: Resource Planning and Scheduling* (Prentice-Hall, Englewood Cliffs, NJ, 1963)
5. S. Tao, Z.S. Dong, Multi-mode resource-constrained project scheduling problem with alternative project structures. Comput. Ind. Eng. **125**, 333–347 (2018)
6. F. Wei, Ericsson, research on resource allocation of new product R&D projects under multi-project environment. J. Manag. Eng. **19**(S1), 6–10 (2005)
7. C.Y. Lee, L. Lei, Multiple-project scheduling with controllable project duration and hard resource constraint: some solvable cases. Ann. Oper. Res. **102**(1–4), 287–307 (2001)
8. A.P. Van Der Merwe, Multi-project management-organizational structure and control. Int. J. Proj. Manag. **15**(4), 223–233 (1997)
9. P. Eskerod, A. Jerbrant, The resource allocation syndrome: the prime challenge of multi-project management? Int. J. Proj. Manag. **21**(6), 403–409 (2003)
10. A. Lova, C. Maroto, P. Tormos, A multicriteria heuristic method to improve resource allocation in multiproject scheduling. Eur. J. Oper. Res. **127**(2), 408–424 (2000)
11. J.F. Goncalves, J.J.M. Mendes, M.G.C. Resende, A genetic algorithm for the resource constrained multi-project scheduling problem. Eur. J. Oper. Res. **189**(3), 1171–1190 (2008)
12. S.C. Graves, A review of production scheduling. Oper. Res. **29**(4), 646–675 (1981)
13. V. Van de Vonder, E. Demeulemeester, W. Herroelen, Proactive heuristic procedures for robust project scheduling: an experimental analysis. Eur. J. Oper. Res. **189**(3), 723–733 (2008)
14. M.E. Bruni, P. Beraldi, F. Guerriero, et al., A heuristic approach for resource constrained project scheduling with uncertain activity durations. Comput. Oper. Res. **38**(9), 1305–1318 (2011)
15. M.E. Bruni, L. Di Puglia Pugliese, P. Beraldi, et al., An adjustable robust optimization model for the resource-constrained project scheduling problem with uncertain activity durations. Omega **71**, 66–84 (2018)
16. M.E. Bruni, L. Di Puglia Pugliese, P. Beraldi, et al., A computational study of exact approaches for the adjustable robust resource-constrained projects scheduling problem. Comput. Oper. Res. **99**, 178–190 (2018)
17. R. Leus, W. Herroelen, Stability and resource allocation in project planning. IIE Trans. **36**(7), 667–682 (2004)
18. M. Brčić, M. Katić, N. Hlupić, Planning horizons based proactive rescheduling for stochastic resource-constrained project scheduling problems. Eur. J. Oper. Res. **273**, 58–66 (2019)
19. D.S. Yamashita, V.A. Armentano, M. Laguna, Robust optimization models for project scheduling with resource availability cost. J. Sched. **10**(1), 67–76 (2007)
20. H.C. Xu, X.F. Xu, A cross enterprise project robust scheduling algorithm considering resource reliability. Autom. J. **38**(12), 1–10 (2012)
21. C. Aritigues, R. Leus, F.T. Nobibon, Robust optimization for resource-constrained project scheduling with uncertainty activity durations. Flex. Serv. Manuf. J. **25**(1–2), 175–205 (2013)
22. Y.Y. Shou, *Resource Constrained Multi Project Scheduling Model and Method* (Zhejiang University Press, Hangzhou, 2010)
23. H. Zheng, K. Zheng, H.L. Bai, *Multi Objective Equilibrium Analysis Model for Project Scheduling and Its Application* (Southwestern University of Finance and Economics Press, Chengdu, 2013)
24. Y.Y. Shou, W. Wang, Project scheduling strategy based on robust optimization model genetic algorithm. Manag. Eng. J **23**(4), 148–152 (2009)
25. L.H. Yang, D. Yang, Genetic algorithm based resource constrained project scheduling optimization. Manag. Sci. **21**(4), 60–68 (2008)

Chapter 5
Study on Home Care Scheduling with Considerations of the Patient Satisfaction and Operation Costs

Home care means care provided at home by family members or professional carers to people who otherwise might require institutional care. The promotion and implementation of home care systems significantly improved public health and lowered medical expenses. Home care systems, which originated in developed countries, have been introduced and piloted in China in recent years. This section is focused on the home care provided by professionals. First, the status and characteristics of the home care systems in China and abroad are introduced. Then, some operational issues in home care system are explored. More specifically, aiming at improving patient satisfaction and lowering operational costs, home care resource allocation and task scheduling problems are studied in depth. The optimisation model and its algorithm are proposed and analysed systematically. Finally, taking a home care system in Shanghai as an example, the effectiveness of the optimisation approach is tested.

5.1 Home Care Systems and Their Scheduling Needs

5.1.1 Home Care Practices Abroad

Home care systems originated in the United Kingdom in the nineteenth century and were gradually accepted by public after World War II. Since then, the construction of social medical and health systems and welfare systems in the United Kingdom has rapidly advanced. Thereafter, the home care systems were adopted and established in Australia, Germany, Canada, the United States, and other countries.

In the United Kingdom, family doctors (i.e., general practitioners) sign contracts with local health departments through the Family Doctors Association to practice individually, cooperatively, or collectively. Every resident over the age of 16 is eligible to freely choose a family doctor registered in their local area, and residents under the age of 16 are registered by their parents or guardians. Each family doctor is responsible for medical treatment and prevention for 1800–2500 residents, and residents must first go to their family doctor for treatment when sick. Those who have intractable diseases or require hospitalisation must have a referral from their family doctor before being transferred to a specialist hospital or a higher-level hospital for treatment. Under special circumstances, a family doctor may also arrange home visits by a specialist for their patients.

Most general practitioners in the United Kingdom are independent contractors who provide general medical services through the National Health Service (NHS) in accordance with the terms of a service contract [1, 2]. The United Kingdom has implemented a strict admission system for general practitioners. To become a general practitioner, the applicant must first receive at least 5 years of medical school education followed by 3 years of systematic training in general practice, pass an examination to obtain a general practitioner certificate, and be registered as a member of the Royal Society of Medicine. Doctors with extensive clinical experience also must pass examinations to obtain a general practitioner certificate after 1 year of training on general medicine. Such high standards allow general practitioners to be fully capable of diagnosing and treating common diseases in community and to earn the trust of the residents of community.

Although specific practice details vary among countries, home care systems in developed countries have the following characteristics:

1. Contracted Services Provided by Home Care Workers to Residents

In home care systems, various countries have established a mechanism by which home care workers sign contracts with residents and have clear regulations regarding the number of contracted residents served by a home care worker, i.e., approximately 2000 (for example, 2500 in the United Kingdom and 2300 in the United States) [3–5].

2. Community First Contact Care Requirement

Community first contact care is a very important basic policy of home care systems. Except in emergency cases, patients must first be seen by home care workers for initial diagnosis and treatment, and only in the event of difficult-to-treat diseases or serious illnesses requiring hospitalisation will patients be referred to higher-level hospitals [6–9].

3. Prepaid Per Capita for Health Service Funds

Based on the number of contracted residents, the health management department allocates annual medical and health service funds in advance to home care workers, who use and manage the funds autonomously. On this basis, home care workers provide residents with appropriate and effective medical and health services; a certain proportion of the reasonable surplus of health services funds is incorporated into the income of home healthcare workers [10, 11].

4. High Qualifications for Home Care Workers

The requirements for home care practitioners from the beginning of training to professional qualification reviews are very stringent [12]. Home care practitioners in the United Kingdom must have received professional training in general medicine (including rotations in various hospital departments) and be physicians registered with the Royal Society of Medicine; those in the Netherlands must have a good medical education background and have completed 3 years of standardised clinical practice training.

5. Services that Cover all Aspects of Health Management

In addition to providing primary care services, home care workers in the United Kingdom also provide home visit services for people with limited mobility and are responsible for the health care of women, children, middle-aged individuals, and elderly individuals, offering a full range of services that integrate prevention, treatment, healthcare, and rehabilitation for residents, families, and communities.

6. Home Care Workers Provide Integrated and Coordinated Services

Importance is attached to services coordinated among home care workers as well as between home care workers and auxiliary staff such as nurses and pharmacists. The Dutch government encourages home care workers to cooperate with nurses and pharmacists to provide better medical services. Healthcare liaisons are often available in UK clinics to provide specialised services such as foreign language translation and medical assistance, and pharmacists could provide services such as health consultations and blood pressure measurements.

5.1.2 Home Care Practices in China

With the reform of the medical and health system, China's healthcare system is transitioning from specialised services solely provided by hospitals to a combination of general and specialised medical services. Stimulated by relevant policies, pilot home care systems have been initiated in some Chinese cities (e.g., Beijing, Shenzhen, and Shanghai).

1. Beijing: Taking Tongzhou district, Beijing, as an instance, the Social Security Administration of the Health Bureau of Tongzhou district, Beijing, has been comprehensively promoting and implementing home care services in 19 community health service centres in the district, through which 480 home care workers, nurses, and prevention/control personnel who form 127 community health service teams implement various activities such as outpatient clinics, home visits, publicity and education, and theme days. The relationship between doctors and 314,700 families in the district has been established through various modern communication methods such as mobile phones and the Internet.
2. Shenzhen: Shenzhen has established a new medical and health care service model with home care workers as the core personnel responsible for care, community health service centres as technical support, and the health management of community residents and their families as the work content. Community health

Table 5.1 The population that served by the Anting Community Hospital

Population type	Retired cadres	Certified persons with disabilities	Elderly individuals	Patients with hypertension	Patients with diabetes	Patients with tumours
Number	25	1614	225	13,447	3061	1232

service centres provide contracted services through family doctors; the medical staff help residents choose family doctors, register, select personalised services and sign service contracts. Residents who have selected a family doctor can make an appointment online or by phone and go to a community health centre to receive services at the appointment time or schedule a home visit.

3. Shanghai: Shanghai has formed a community health service model that features a "community health service centre + general practitioner service team." Below, the family doctor service model of Anting Community Hospital in Jiading district, Shanghai, is described in detail.

Anting Township of Jiading district is located at the junction of Shanghai and Jiangsu province; it has a total area of 89.28 km^2, a registered population of 85,000, and a permanent population of nearly 250,000 residing in 37 administrative villages, 16 communities, and 4 farmer villa communities. There are 22 doctors (including general practitioners, doctors of traditional Chinese medicine, public health doctors, and physicians) and approximately 50 nurses at Anting Community Hospital. These personnel are divided into six medical service teams, with two nurses generally assigned for each doctor. In addition, the community hospital divides the entire service area into six regions, each of which is assigned to a medical service team, with each doctor in charge of a certain subregion.

Within the service area of Anting Community Hospital, there is a population in need of medical care, as shown in Table 5.1. At the community hospital, a family doctor office is dedicated to accepting and processing home healthcare service applications. Each patient is assigned to a regional medical team; when a patient needs home healthcare services, he/she can submit an application to the family doctor office and provide some basic information including physical conditions, medical history, and healthcare needs, and the address of family, etc. Then, the office will assign the applicant to the corresponding regional medical team, which in turn assigns a doctor and coordinates detailed arrangements such as specific time and service requirements.

5.1.3 Scheduling Problem in Home Care Services

Home care systems involve complex stakeholders and diverse medical resources. Medical resource shortages can be the main constraint restricting the promotion and application of home care systems. The effectiveness of existing resources can be maximised by establishing the optimal resource scheduling plans through operations research approaches.

1. Key Resources and Parties

To implement home care systems, in addition to government coordination and regulation, the main parties include medical institutions (community hospitals), medical personnel (home care workers), and contracted patients.

(a) Medical Institutions

Medical institutions mainly include community hospitals. When community hospitals participate in home care services, one of their critical concerns is to minimise operating costs. With the development of home care systems, institutions such as drug suppliers, medical testing departments, and third-party logistics may also be involved in the future.

(b) Medical Personnel

Medical personnel mainly include doctors and nurses, who are in charge of patient care in designated regions. Usually, a home care team consists of a doctor, and several nurses will be sent to the patient's home for delivering the home care services. Since medical personnel are the scarcest resources, therefore, the scheduling of medical personnel is very critical to the operations management of home care systems.

(c) Patients

All the residents in the region are contracted patients. Among them, elderly individuals, children, pregnant women, and disabled individuals have a high frequency of medical service needs. The main types of care include basic medical services, care for chronic diseases, and care for special groups. Here, patient satisfaction is the main evaluation index and is affected by many factors, such as care duration and effectiveness.

2. Home Care Service Process and its Scheduling

In practice, the home care service process, i.e., from the application for services to the completion of services, involves five stages: pre-care assessment, health condition diagnosis, care planning, care plan implementation, and care effectiveness evaluation, as shown in Fig. 5.1.

In the planning and implementation stages, the activities involved include allocating medical staff to meet patient requirements based on patient care type and frequency and arranging medical staff to visit patients at homes at scheduled times. This process involves resource allocation and scheduling, e.g., the allocation of medical staff and the scheduling of care service routes. Given that there are limited medical resources, reasonably scheduling resources and lowering operating costs under the premise of meeting the needs of patients have become the focus of management.

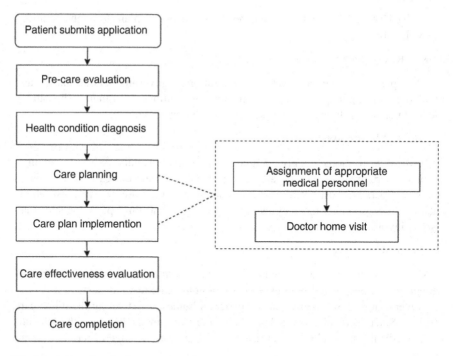

Fig. 5.1 A flow chart for home care services

This chapter focuses on scheduling home care workers in the planning and implementation stages. When patients need home care services, they need to apply to the care centre and provide information regarding the care requested (e.g., service type and frequency of care). Based on patients' needs, the home care centre schedules medical professionals (as a team) who match the patients' care type to provide the requested services. As a result, a home care team needs to deliver a number of home care services for different patients that are randomly located in the region area. Therefore, the care tasks for a home care team should be scheduled for each working day, with the daily working hours not exceeding the specified maximum working hours. Usually, the home care workers must be dispatched from the home healthcare centre and return to the centre after completing all care tasks of the day. To reduce non-value-added activities, the distance travelled between different patients should be minimised.

Based on the above analysis, home care scheduling can be divided into two problems.

Problem 1: Determine the specific home care workers and the date of care for each patient during the planning period. When assigning home care workers, the following three points must be considered: (1) the specialty of the home care worker can satisfy the patient's requirement; (2) the number of dispatched workers cannot exceed the corresponding resource limit; and (3) the number of care services needed by a patient within the planning period can be fulfilled. Here, the optimisation objective is set to minimising the operating costs of the home care centre while considering patient satisfaction.

Problem 2: When the home care workers are determined for each patient, the patients who each home care worker must visit on each working day during the planning period are also determined. Due to the dispersion of residences of patients in need of care every day, specific daily travel routes must be reasonably determined for home care workers. As patients are scattered throughout the region, travel time becomes main non-value-added time (a kind of waste time) for home care workers. Saving travel time can increase the service capacity of the home healthcare centre. Therefore, it is necessary to plan a travel route for each home healthcare worker so that each home healthcare worker uses the shortest amount of time possible to travel to all patients who require services in a day.

5.2   Optimal Modelling Considering Patient Satisfaction and Care Costs

Here, we will construct a bi-objective mixed integer programming model to schedule home care workers by simultaneously considering the operating costs and patient satisfaction. Specifically, the model will consider the needs of patients in terms of the type, frequency, and duration of care services as well as the service limits of home care workers in terms of working hours and working days and ensure the consistency of service by controlling the changing times of home care workers that provide services to the same patient. By combining the interests of both home care centres and patients, the optimisation objectives are to minimise the operating costs of the home care centre and maximise patient satisfaction, to provide the optimal scheduling schemes for home care workers and decision support for home care centres.

Next, we will describe the bi-objective scheduling model as well as the variables and parameters, constraints and optimisation objectives of the model. Thereafter, we will demonstrate the optimisation process for small-scale problems using specific examples to obtain a Pareto curve through the ε-constraint algorithm.

5.2.1   Description of the Bi-objective Model

Given that home care operations involve long-term processes that require multi-party cooperation, in which both home care centres and patients play important roles, finding a balance between operating costs and patient satisfaction and constructing a bi-objective model for home care worker scheduling are substantial tasks.

In the bi-objective model, operating costs mainly refer to the costs incurred by home care centre when providing home care services, including travel costs corresponding to travel time, care costs corresponding to care duration, and penalty costs corresponding to home care workers' overtime. Patient satisfaction is affected by many factors. Here, it is measured by the degree of completion of each patient's required care duration. The parameters, variables, constraints, and objective functions of the model are discussed below.

1. Model Parameters and Variables

The optimisation model is a mixed integer programming model. And the involved subscripts and sets, parameters, and variables are described in Tables 5.2, 5.3, and 5.4, respectively.

2. Model Constraints

At most, one visit per day can be scheduled for each patient, which is expressed in Constraint (5.1).

$$\sum_{w \in W_j^d} v_j^{wd} \leq 1, \; j \in N', d \in D \tag{5.1}$$

To ensure consistency of medical services, the changing times of home care workers assigned to a patient during the planning period should be minimised. Here, the changing times of home care workers is limited to U, as shown in Constraint (5.2).

$$\sum_{w \in W_j} u_j^w \leq U, \; j \in N' \tag{5.2}$$

Normally, home care workers work approximately 8–10 h/day. If they work overtime, the home care centre will bear additional fines. In this regard, the auxiliary

Table 5.2 Description of subscripts and sets of the model

Subscript and set	Description
i, j	ID number of the patient in need of home care, $i, j \in N'$, $N' = \{1, 2, \ldots, n-1\}$
w	ID number of the home care worker, $w \in W$
d	Date within the planning period, $d \in D$
N	Set of nodes, i.e., $N = N' \cup \{n\}$, where N' is the set of patient locations and $\{n\}$ is the location of home care Centre.
D	Set of working days
W	Set of home care workers
W^d	Set of home care workers working on day d
W_j	Set of home care workers who meet the type requirement for patient j
W_j^d	Set of home care workers who work on day d and meet the type requirement for patient j

Table 5.3 Parameters of the model

Parameter	Description
U	The maximum allowable changing times of home care workers assigned to a patient in terms of care consistency
r_j	Frequency of care services requested by patient j during the planning period
g_j	Duration of care required by patient j
S	Set of optional care durations offered by the care Centre, $S = \{s_1, s_2, \ldots, s_f\}$, $f = |S|$
L^w	Daily working hours for home care worker w (between 8–9 h)
t_{ij}	Travel time between patients i and j, which is used to calculate the travel cost
C_w	Hourly wage of home care worker w: $c_w = (a + bT^w)$, where T^w is the type of home care worker w, a is the basic hourly wage and is a constant, and b is an adjustment factor and is also a constant
p	Penalty that the home care Centre must pay when the care worker works overtime
e, m	e is the basic satisfaction coefficient, and m is an adjustment factor, both of which are constants

Table 5.4 Variables of the model

Variable	Description
v_j^{wd}	Binary variable; 1 if home care worker w visits patient j on day d, and 0 otherwise
s_j^{wd}	Duration of care provided by home care worker w to patient j on day d. if w visits j on d, i.e., $v_j^{wd} = 1$, then $s_j^{wd} \in S$; otherwise, $s_j^{wd} = 0$
x_{ij}^{wd}	Binary variable; 1 if home care worker w visits patient j immediately after visiting patient i on day d, and 0 otherwise
u_j^w	Auxiliary variable; 1 if home care worker w visits patient j, and 0 otherwise, i.e., $u_j^w = \max_{d \in D} v_j^{wd}$
y_{ij}^{wd}	Auxiliary variable used to avoid loops. If home care worker w visits patient j immediately after visiting patient i on day d, then this variable represents the number of patients who w must visit after visiting patient i.
a^{wd}	Auxiliary variable that represents the overtime hours worked by home care worker w on day d that exceeds L^w. If the worker does not work overtime, then the value is 0.

variable a^{wd} is introduced to calculate daily overtime hours worked by each home care worker, and the overtime penalty is reflected in the objective function.

$$a^{wd} \geq \sum_{i,j \in N, i \neq j} x_{ij}^{wd} t_{ij} + \sum_{j \in N'} s_j^{wd} - L^w, \; d \in D, w \in W^d \quad (5.3)$$

During the planning period, if a patient requires multiple visits, the home care centre must schedule the corresponding number of visits for the patient, as shown in Constraints (5.4):

$$\sum_{d\in D}\sum_{w\in W_j^d} v_j^{wd} = r_j, \ \ j \in N' \tag{5.4}$$

Providing patients with care based on an expected duration is considered meeting their basic needs. If more time can be provided, patient satisfaction can improve further. Here, the extra amount of time of each patient is calculated using Constraints (5.5) and (5.6), and accordingly, patient satisfaction is calculated in the objective function. Constraint (5.5) indicates that if home care worker w visits patient j on day d, the duration of the visit should not be shorter than the patient's expected duration; Constraint (5.6) indicates that the care time variable is 0 when no visit occurs.

$$\left(s_j^{wd} - g_j\right) - M\left(v_j^{wd} - 1\right) \geq 0, \ \ d \in D, j \in N', w \in W_j^d \tag{5.5}$$

$$s_j^{wd} \leq M v_j^{wd}, \ d \in D, j \in N', w \in W_j^d \tag{5.6}$$

When scheduling the daily routes for home care workers, the continuity of the route should be ensured, and loops should be avoided. Constraint (5.7) represents the continuity between nodes visited by home care workers, and Constraints (5.8)–(5.10) restrict the occurrence of loops.

$$\sum_{i\in N, j\neq i} x_{ij}^{wd} = \sum_{i\in N, i\neq j} x_{ji}^{wd}, \ j \in N', d \in D, w \in W_j^d \tag{5.7}$$

$$\sum_{j\in N'} y_{nj}^{wd} = \sum_{j\in N'} v_j^{wd}, w \in W^d, d \in D \tag{5.8}$$

$$\sum_{i\in N, i\neq j} y_{ij}^{wd} - \sum_{i\in N, i\neq j} y_{ji}^{wd} = v_j^{wd}, \ j \in N', d \in D, w \in W^d \tag{5.9}$$

$$y_{ij}^{wd} \leq n x_{ij}^{wd}, \ \{i \neq j\} \in N, d \in D, w \in W^d \tag{5.10}$$

The home care centre must control the consistency of various decisions with regard to assigning home care workers to patients and developing daily visit plans and travel routes for home care workers. Constraints (5.11) and (5.12) indicate that the daily visit plan is developed based on home care workers assignment for each patient. Constraint (5.13) ensures that the daily visit plan is consistent with the arranged route. Constraints (5.14) and (5.15) indicate the route for the home care worker w who is assigned to visit patient j.

$$M u_j^w \geq \sum_{d\in D} v_j^{wd}, \ j \in N', w \in W_j \tag{5.11}$$

$$u_j^w \leq \sum_{d \in D} v_j^{wd}, \ j \in N', w \in W_j \tag{5.12}$$

$$\sum_{i \in N, j \neq i} x_{ij}^{wd} = v_j^{wd}, \ j \in N', d \in D, w \in W_j^d \tag{5.13}$$

$$\sum_{i \in N} \sum_{d \in D} x_{ij}^{wd} + M\left(1 - u_j^w\right) \geq 1, \ j \in N', w \in W_j^d \tag{5.14}$$

$$\sum_{i \in N} \sum_{d \in D} x_{ij}^{wd} - u_j^w \leq 0, \ j \in N', w \in W_j^d \tag{5.15}$$

The value ranges for the variables introduced in the model are restrained as follows:

$$u_j^w \in \{0, 1\}, \ j \in N', w \in W_j \tag{5.16}$$

$$x_{ij}^{wd} \in \{0, 1\}, y_{ij}^{wd} \geq 0, \ \{i \neq j\} \in N, d \in D, w \in W_j^d \tag{5.17}$$

$$v_j^{wd} \in \{0, 1\}, s_j^{wd} \in S \cup \{0\}, \ j \in N', d \in D, w \in W_j^d \tag{5.18}$$

$$a^{wd} \geq 0, \ d \in D, w \in W^d \tag{5.19}$$

3. Objective Functions

The bi-objective optimisation model includes the minimisation of care centre operating costs and the maximisation of patient satisfaction.

Objective 1 in Eq. (5.20) considers the salary of home care workers for providing medical services and the fines borne by the home care centre for home care workers who worked overtime. The salary of home care workers is calculated as the product of the hourly wage and the sum of the service duration and travel time. Because the salaries of different home care workers vary, a linear relation with the type of home care worker ($a + bT^w$) is used to reflect the salary difference. When home care workers work overtime, the home care centre must provide overtime subsidies, which is calculated by multiplying the penalty coefficient p and the overtime hours.

Objective 2 in Eq. (5.21), the patient overall satisfaction is calculated using the linear equation. Patient satisfaction includes two parts: basic satisfaction and extra satisfaction. If the service duration is equal to the patient's expectations, basic patient satisfaction is achieved. If the service duration exceeds the patient's expectations, the patient has extra satisfaction.

$$\min Z_1 = \sum_{d \in D} \sum_{w \in W} \left\{ \left(\sum_{i, \ j \in N, \ j \neq i} x_{ij}^{wd} t_{ij} + \sum_{j \in N'} s_j^{wd} \right) \left(a + bT^w \right) + p a^{wd} \right\} \tag{5.20}$$

$$\max Z_2 = \sum_{j \in N'} \left\{ e + m \cdot \left(\sum_{d \in D} \sum_{w \in W_j^d} s_j^{wd} - r_j g_j \right) \right\} \qquad (5.21)$$

5.2.2　Solving the Model Using the ε-Constraint Algorithm

The ε-constraint algorithm has been widely used to solve multi-objective optimisation problems [13, 14] and is also very effective for solving bi-objective optimisation problems [15]. In this section, we will first introduce the concept of the ε-constraint algorithm and then illustrate the solution process using an example.

1. Process of Solving Non-dominated Solutions

Pareto dominance is a key concept of the ε-constraint algorithm and describes the relationship between feasible solutions. When solving a multi-objective minimisation problem, solution A is considered better than solution B only when $f_i(A) \leq f_i(B)$ and there is at least one objective i, such that $f_i(A) < f_i(B)$, where $i = 1$, $2, \ldots, m$, with m being the number of objectives. All non-dominated solutions like solution A in the objective space form the Pareto front.

The key to solving a bi-objective problem using the ε-constraint algorithm is to convert one of the objectives into a ε-constraint and add it to the programming model and then to gradually reduce the ε value and solve a series of single-objective optimisation models containing the ε-constraint to obtain the corresponding non-dominated solutions.

In this optimisation problem, $m = 2$, and the second objective is to maximise patient satisfaction. Therefore, the second objective is multiplied by "-1" to convert it into a minimisation problem to simplify the process of solving the non-dominated solutions,

i.e., objective 2 becomes $\min Z_2 = (-1) \cdot \sum_{j \in N'} \left\{ e + m \cdot \left(\sum_{d \in D} \sum_{w \in W_j^d} s_j^{wd} - r_j g_j \right) \right\}$.

Figure 5.2 illustrates the specific process of solving a bi-objective optimisation problem using the ε-constraint algorithm. In which, (f_1^I, f_2^I) and (f_1^N, f_2^N) are the ideal point and the worst point of the bi-objective problem, respectively. By sequentially solving the single-objective optimisation problem corresponding to each objective in the bi-objective problem, the optimal values f_1^I and f_2^I are obtained, which form the ideal point. The value of one objective is solved by using the optimal value of the other objective as the constraint; therefore, the worst value for the former objective is obtained; the worst values f_1^N and f_2^N are sequentially obtained, which form the worst point. When solving the problem, the second objective (patient satisfaction) is converted into a constraint to solve the optimisation problem of objective 1 (operating cost). During the iteration, the value of ε is decreased by Δ in each iterative step, and Δ denotes the satisfaction increment corresponding to the

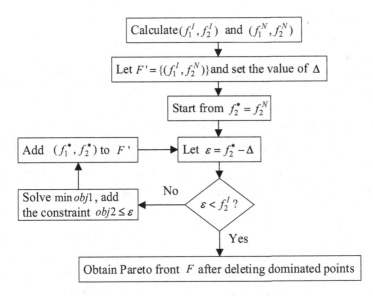

Fig. 5.2 Flow chart for the solution process of the ε-constraint algorithm

hourly care service provided. As patient satisfaction approaches the ideal point from the worst point, a series of corresponding operating cost values are generated. As a result, a series of points corresponding to the two objectives, i.e., operating cost and patient satisfaction, will form the Pareto front.

2. An Example

Here, a small-scale numerical example with a planning period of 5 days is constructed and solved in CPLEX 12.6. The specific optimisation processes are elaborated to illustrate the effectiveness of the ε-constraint algorithm in solving the bi-objective model.

The example includes five home care workers with three different specialties. The working days and working hours of each home care worker are listed in Table 5.5. The optional service durations offered by the home care centre are $\{0.25, 0.5, 0.75, 1.0, 1.25, 1.5\}$. The specific care needs of eight patients are provided in Table 5.6. To ensure consistency regarding the provision of care services, the changing times of home care workers assigned to one patient during the planning period cannot exceed two. The base salary coefficient for home care worker is 210, the adjustment coefficient related to the type of home care worker is 30, and the penalty coefficient for overtime hours worked is 500. The basic satisfaction coefficient is 70, and the hourly adjustment coefficient for extra services is 24.

Based on calculations, the above example has the ideal point $(f_1^I, f_2^I) = (9477, 1302)$ and the worst point $(f_1^N, f_2^N) = (20541, 534)$. Using patient satisfaction as a constraint and cost minimisation as the optimisation objective, the iteration starts from the extreme point $(9477, 534)$, and the Pareto front consisting of

Table 5.5 Information for home healthcare workers in a home healthcare centre

Home care worker ID	1	2	3	4	5
Home care worker type	3	1	2	1	1
Working days	1,3,4,5	2,3,4	1,2,4,5	2,3,5	2,3,4,5
Working hours	8	8	8	8	8

Table 5.6 Patient care needs

Patient ID	1	2	3	4	5	6	7	8
Frequency	1	3	3	1	3	3	3	3
Type	2	1	3	1	3	2	3	3
Duration	0.90	0.65	0.67	0.88	0.34	0.46	0.69	0.98

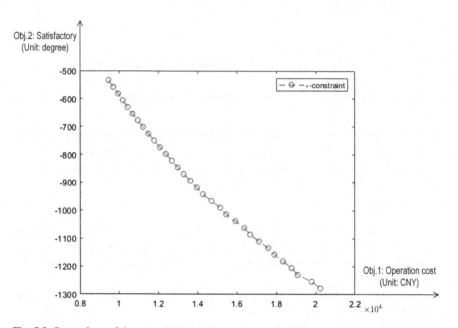

Fig. 5.3 Pareto front of the numerical example

32 non-dominated solutions (see Fig. 5.3) is obtained (see columns 2 and 4 of Table 5.7 for detail). To facilitate analysis, the values for satisfaction are converted to negative values. The numbers listed in columns 3 and 5 are the gaps between the solutions and their respective ideal values. As patient satisfaction gradually increases and approaches the ideal value, the gap between the calculated cost value and its ideal value increases. In particular, when satisfaction takes the maximum value, the cost increases by 113.58% compared to the ideal value. In comparison, when the cost takes the minimum value, the satisfaction decreases by 58.99% compared to the ideal value.

Table 5.7 Summary of non-dominated solutions

Solution ID	Objective 1		Objective 2	
	Cost	ΔOpt1	Satisfaction	ΔOpt1
(1) min Obj. 1	9477	+0.00%	534	−58.99%
(2)Obj. 2 ≥ 558	9717	+2.53%	558	−57.14%
(3)Obj. 2 ≥ 582	9957	+5.06%	582	−55.30%
(4)Obj. 2 ≥ 606	10,197	+7.60%	606	−53.46%
(5)Obj. 2 ≥ 630	10,437	+10.13%	630	−51.61%
(6)Obj. 2 ≥ 654	10,684	+12.74%	654	−49.77%
(7)Obj. 2 ≥ 678	10,954	+15.59%	678	−47.93%
(8)Obj. 2 ≥ 702	11,224	+18.43%	702	−46.08%
(9)Obj. 2 ≥ 726	11,494	+21.28%	726	−44.24%
(10)Obj. 2 ≥ 750	11,794	+24.45%	750	−42.40%
(11)Obj. 2 ≥ 774	12,094	+27.61%	774	−40.55%
(12)Obj. 2 ≥ 798	12,394	+30.78%	798	−38.71%
(13)Obj. 2 ≥ 822	12,695	+33.96%	822	−36.87%
(14)Obj. 2 ≥ 846	12,997	+37.14%	846	−35.02%
(15)Obj. 2 ≥ 870	13,297	+40.31%	870	−33.18%
(16)Obj. 2 ≥ 894	13,636	+43.89%	894	−31.34%
(17)Obj. 2 ≥ 918	13,976	+47.47%	918	−29.49%
(18)Obj. 2 ≥ 942	14,276	+50.64%	942	−27.65%
(19)Obj. 2 ≥ 966	14,720	+55.32%	966	−25.81%
(20)Obj. 2 ≥ 990	15,164	+60.01%	990	−23.96%
(21)Obj. 2 ≥ 1014	15,464	+63.17%	1014	−22.12%
(22)Obj. 2 ≥ 1038	15,935	+68.14%	1038	−20.28%
(23)Obj. 2 ≥ 1062	16,379	+72.83%	1062	−18.43%
(24)Obj. 2 ≥ 1086	16,679	+75.99%	1086	−16.59%
(25)Obj. 2 ≥ 1110	17,123	+80.68%	1110	−14.75%
(26)Obj. 2 ≥ 1134	17,595	+85.66%	1134	−12.90%
(27)Obj. 2 ≥ 1158	17,895	+88.83%	1158	−11.06%
(28)Obj. 2 ≥ 1182	18,339	+93.51%	1182	−9.22%
(29)Obj. 2 ≥ 1206	18,783	+98.20%	1206	−7.37%
(30)Obj. 2 ≥ 1230	19,083	+101.36%	1230	−5.53%
(31)Obj. 2 ≥ 1254	19,797	+108.90%	1254	−3.69%
(32)Obj. 2 ≥ 1278	20,241	+113.58%	1278	−1.84%
Ideal	9477	+0.00%	1302	−0.00%
Nadir	20,541	+116.75%	534	−58.99%

The problem studied here is an NP-hard problem (an extension of the travelling salesman problem-TSP). Due to computational complexity, even solving the above small-scale problem would still take a very long computation time. For this reason, it is necessary to develop a faster algorithm for processing larger-scale problems in practical applications. Therefore, a heuristic algorithm is designed in the next section to obtain non-dominated solutions for large-scale problems within a reasonable timeframe.

5.3　Design of a Fast Algorithm and Its Numerical Analysis

To quickly obtain an optimal solution for the bi-objective problem of actual home care worker scheduling, in this section, two heuristic algorithms, i.e., NSGA-II and the random assignment algorithm, are developed and tested through numerical analyses.

5.3.1　Flowchart of the NSGA-II Algorithm

Non-dominated sorting genetic algorithm II (NSGA-II) is an evolutionary algorithm that integrates fast non-dominated sorting method and the elitist keeping strategy and thus can effectively solve multi-objective optimisation problems [16]. The procedure of this algorithm is shown in Algorithm 1. In this algorithm, the problem parameters and algorithm parameters are first entered. In which, the algorithm parameters include the population size pop, the number of generations gen and the crossover and mutation probabilities in genetic operations. The parent population P_0 is randomly generated by INITIAL _ POPULATION. P_{t-1} represents the parent chromosomes of the $(t-1)$th generation, and Q_{t-1} represents the offspring produced by the parents (referring to the genetic operation in Line 14). R_t represents a combination of the parent chromosomes and the offspring chromosomes. The individuals in R_t are sorted to different non-dominated levels F through NON _ DOMINATED _ SORT using the elitist keeping strategy. All individuals in the first $(i-1)$ non-dominated levels and K individuals selected from F_i form P_t. For details of NSGA-II, please refer to [16].

Algorithm 1　Procedure of the NSGA-II algorithm

Input: Problem parameters, algorithm parameters
Output: Non-dominated solutions
1: $P_0 \leftarrow$ INITIAL _ POPULATION();
2: $Q_0 \leftarrow \varnothing$;
3: **for** t $\leftarrow$ 1 : gen **do**
4:　　$R_t \leftarrow P_{t-1} \cup Q_{t-1}$;
5:　　F $\leftarrow$ NON _ DOMINATED _ SORT(R_t);
6:　　$P_t \leftarrow \varnothing$;
7:　　i $\leftarrow$ 1;
8:　　**while** $|P_t| + |F_i| \leq pop$ **do**
9:　　　　$P_t \leftarrow P_t \cup F_i$;
10:　　　i $\leftarrow$ i + 1;
11:　　**end while**
12:　　K $\leftarrow pop - |P_t|$;
13:　　$P_t \leftarrow P_t \cup$ SELECTION(P_t, F_i, K);
14:　　$Q_t \leftarrow$ GENETIC _ OPERATORS(P_t);
15: **end for**

As follows, the solution transformation, initial population generation, and genetic operators related to the algorithm are described in detail.

1. Solution Transformation

The feasible solutions for the studied problem contain three aspects of information: (1) the allocation of home care workers to patients, i.e., v_j^{wd}, indicating whether home care worker w visits patient j on day d; (2) the duration of service provided by the home care worker for the patient, i.e., s_j^{wd}; and (3) the daily route for each home care worker, i.e., x_{ij}^{wd}. The value of s_j^{wd} can be a positive real number selected from the optional set S only when home care worker w visits patient j on day d. Otherwise, it should be 0. Therefore, v_j^{wd} is valued at 1 if the value of s_j^{wd} is greater than zero, and 0 otherwise. The travel route decision is related to the patients to be cared for by the home care workers on day d and thus it is an extension of the TSP. When the service duration s_j^{wd} is determined, the daily route of home care workers can be planned accordingly. In summary, decision for the problem can be transformed into the decision for service duration.

Because the travel path decision is an NP-hard problem, it is impossible to obtain the optimal route in polynomial time. Therefore, the greedy algorithm is introduced here to obtain the near-optimal route; the detailed procedure is shown in Algorithm 2. Each route starts and ends at the home care centre. In each iteration, the patients who have already been cared for are removed from the set to ensure that each patient is scheduled for care at most once per day and that all patients in the set can be scheduled for care. The performance of the algorithm has been verified, with a worst-case ratio of 1.25 [17].

Algorithm 2 Framework of the nearest neighbour search algorithm

---

Input: The set of patients (N) to be visited by home healthcare worker w on day d, and the distance matrix D

Output: Near-optimal path P

1: $num \leftarrow |N|$;

2: $P_1 \leftarrow$ Agency;(%origin of the path)

3: $N \leftarrow N\backslash\{P_1\}$;

4: **for** $j \leftarrow 2 : num$ **do**

5:    $P_j \leftarrow$ MIN _ DISTANCE(P_{j-1}, N, D);

6:    $N \leftarrow N\backslash\{P_j\}$;

7: **end for**

8: $P_{num+1} \leftarrow P_1$;

---

2. Initial Population Generation

The initial population size is equal to the parameter *pop* in the algorithm, and the specific process of generating the initial population is shown in Algorithm 3. A feasibility test is performed at each step when processing constraints such as patient needs, home care worker specialty, and working days. When the home care worker or the service duration is optional, random selection is used to ensure a diversity of initial solutions.

Algorithm 3 Framework of the initial solution generation

Input: Problem parameters, initial population size *pop*
Output: Initial solution set
1: **for** i ← 1 : *pop* **do**
2:   **for** *j* ← 1 : *patient _ size* **do**
3:     *doc _ num* ← 0;
4:     **for** w ← 1 : *doc _ size* **do**
5:       **if** *doc _ type*(w) = *patient _ type*(*j*) and *doc _ num* < *U* **then**
6:         get working days *doc _ day* of doc w for patient j;
7:         *doc _ num* ← *doc _ num* + 1;
8:       **end if**
9:     **end for**
10:    [*row, col*] ← *Find*(*doc _ day*);
11:    *doc _ day _* choose ← ∅;
12:    **while** *Length*(*doc _ day _ choose*) < *r*(*j*) **do**
13:      *rp* = *Randi*([1, *Length*(*row*)], 1, 1);
14:      *doc* ← *row*(*rp*);
15:      *day* ← *col*(*rp*)
16:      **if** *day*thcolumn of *doc _ day _ choose* is empty **then**
17:        *doc _ day _ choose*(*doc, day*) = *Randi*([*g*(*j*), *maxg*], 1, 1);
18:      **end if**
19:    **end while**
20: **end for**
21: **end for**

3. Genetic Operators

Crossover and mutation are common operators for producing offspring in evolutionary algorithms. Here, the simulated binary crossover and polynomial mutation are used as genetic operators for real number encoding.

During crossover, two individuals are randomly selected as parents to produce two offspring by mating with a crossover probability of P_r. The crossover can occur for each variable in the chromosome. The kth variable in the chromosome of offspring i is expressed as $c_{i, k}$:

$$c_{1,k} = \frac{1}{2}\left[(1 - \beta_k)p_{1,k} + (1 + \beta_k)p_{2,k}\right] \tag{5.22}$$

$$c_{2,k} = \frac{1}{2}\left[(1 + \beta_k)p_{1,k} + (1 - \beta_k)p_{2,k}\right] \tag{5.23}$$

where $p_{i, k}$ is the kth variable of parent chromosome i. $\beta \geq 0$ is a random number generated based on a specific distribution and calculated as follows: (1) when

$0 \leq \beta \leq 1$, then $0 \leq u \leq 0.5$, and $\beta(u) = (2u)^{\frac{1}{(\varphi_c+1)}}$; (2) when $\beta > 1$, then $0.5 < u < 1$, and $\beta(u) = 1/[2(1-u)]^{\frac{1}{(\varphi_c+1)}}$. Here, u is a random number that follows the normal distribution and $u \in (0, 1)$, and φ_c is the distribution index of crossover [16].

To ensure the diversity of offspring, the mutation operation is performed in the evolutionary algorithm with a probability of P_m. Polynomial mutation is used here, as detailed in the following equation:

$$c_k = p_k + \left(p_k^u - p_k^l\right)\delta_k \tag{5.24}$$

where p_k^u and p_k^l are the upper and lower bounds of the kth decision variable, respectively; δ_k is the mutation index calculated using the following polynomial distribution, with r_k being a random number following the normal distribution and φ_m being the mutation distribution index: (1) when $0 < r_k < 0.5$, $\delta_k = (2r_k)^{\frac{1}{\varphi_m+1}} - 1$; (2) when $0.5 \leq r_k < 1$, $\delta_k = 1 - [2(1-r_k)]^{\frac{1}{\varphi_m+1}}$.

The newly generated offspring must pass the feasibility test before they can be subjected to non-dominated sorting. The feasibility test mainly includes the following two steps: (1) the allocation of home care workers to patients must meet the care needs of patients and the constraint on the working days of home care workers; and (2) the service duration must be within the optional time range provided by the home care centre. After each crossover and mutation operations, the offspring must first undergo the feasibility test, and if not feasible, a sufficiently large penalty is added to the fitness function so that it will be eliminated in the next evolution.

5.3.2   Framework of the Random Assignment Algorithm

Because NSGA-II is not stable under different parameter settings and there is a significant increase in time for solving large-scale problems, it is necessary to design additional algorithms to overcome these limitations. Here, a constructive heuristic algorithm based on the characteristics of the problem, i.e., the random assignment algorithm, is presented. When using this algorithm, home care workers, service days, and service duration for each patient are randomly generated within feasible ranges. The specific flowchart is shown in Algorithm 4. A is an algorithm parameter representing the number of random iterations, and its value is set to 20 based on preliminary testing. The parameter setting for the random assignment algorithm is more concise than that for NSGA-II, thus reducing the influence of parameter setting on algorithm effectiveness.

Algorithm 4 Framework of the random assignment algorithm

Input: Problem parameters, number of iterations
Output: Non-dominated solution set
1: **for** k ← 1 : *type* **do**
2:    **for** i ← 1 : *patient _ size* **do**(%classify patients on required types)
3:      **if** *patient _ type* = k **then**
4:        sort patient i to the *patient _ request _ type*;
5:      **end if**
6:    **end for**
7:    **for** w ← 1 : *doc _ size* **do** (%classify docs based on doc types)
8:      **if** *doc _ type* = k **then**
9:        sort doctor w to the *doc _ type*;
10:     **end if**
11:    **end for**
12: **end for**
13: A ← 20;
14: *total _ obj* ← ∅;
15: **for** a ← 1 : A **do**
16:    **for** k ← 1 : *type* **do** (%assign patients to satisfied docs randomly)
17:      **for** j ← 1 : *length(patient _ request _ type)* **do**
18:        **if** *length(doc _ type)* ≥ U **then**
19:          randomly choose U different docs, *doc _ for _ patient*;
20:        **else**
21:          choose U docs with $U - length(doc _ type)$ random repetition, get *doc _ for _ patient*;
22:        **end if**
23:        choose $r(j)$ docs from *doc _ for _ patient*, get *patient _ of _ doc*; (%doc with the minimum workload has priority)
24:      **end for**
25:    **end for**
26:    **for** w ← 1 : *doc _ size* **do** (%arrange service days for patients)
27:      **for** j ← 1 : *length(patient _ of _ doc)* **do**
28:        sort patients in *patient _ of _ doc* based on the working days of w, ensuring no overlap of arrangements, get *doc _ day*;
29:        *travel _ route* = *NEAREST _ NEIGHBOUR* $(doc, day, dis _ matrix)$;
30:        $s_j^{wd} = \max\left\{g_j, \min\{S\}\right\}$;
31:      **end for**
32:    **end for**
33:    calculate *cost* $ *satis.*, add solution to *total _ obj*;
34:    **for** d ← 1 : *day* **do**
35:      **for** w ← 1 : *doc _ size* **do**
36:        **for** j ← 1 : *patient _ size* **do**
37:          **while** $s_j^{wd} < S_{max}$ **do**
38:            $s_j^{wd} ← s_j^{wd} + 1$;
39:            calculate *cost* & *satis.*, add solution to *total _ obj*

(continued)

40	**end while**
41:	**end for**
42:	**end for**
43:	**end for**
44: end for	

5.3.3 Numerical Analysis

To verify the effectiveness of the algorithms, several numerical examples of different scales are constructed for calculation and comparison. The NSGA-II and random assignment algorithms are implemented in MATLAB 2014 on a computer with an Intel 3.30 GHz CPU and 4.00 GB RAM, and the ε-constraint algorithm is implemented in CPLEX 12.6. The unit for the computation time shown in the table is CPU time.

1. Data Generation

The data used in the numerical examples can be divided into three categories: patient care needs, information for home care workers, and evaluation coefficients of objective functions.

(a) Patient Care Needs. Based on family care practices at a community hospital in Shanghai, the home care needs of patients are divided into two main categories: general and traditional Chinese medicine. Therefore, the type of patient care was randomly selected from these two categories when generating data. The frequency of patient care need during the planning period was randomly set to 1, 2, or 3. The upper and lower bounds of the service duration g_j were set to 1.0 and 0.25, respectively, and were randomly generated within this range. In generating the distance matrix, all patients were randomly placed in the Cartesian coordinate system, and the distance between the patients was calculated by the Pythagorean theorem.

(b) Information for Home Care Workers. The care type provided by home care workers was set based on the care needs of the patient, and the specialty of each home care worker was randomly generated. The daily working hours of home care workers ranged from 8 to 10 h, and the working days during the planning period were randomly distributed.

(c) Evaluation Coefficients of Objective Functions. For objective 1, the base salary coefficient was 210, the adjustment coefficient related to the type of home care worker was 30, and the hourly penalty coefficient for overtime hours worked was 500. For objective 2, the basic satisfaction coefficient was 70, and the adjustment coefficient corresponding to extra care hours was 24.

Table 5.8 Scale parameters for the numerical examples

Category	Number of patients	Number of home care workers	Planning period
Small scale	{5, 6, 7, 8}	{2, 3, 4}	{5, 7}
Medium scale	{25,30,35,40}	{8,10,12}	{5, 7}
Large scale	{50,55,60,65}	{14,16,18}	{5, 7}

In addition, the changing times of home care workers assigned to each patient should not exceed 2, and the optional service durations provided by the home care centre was {0.25,0.50,0.75,1.0,1.25,1.5}.

Based on the above rules, a total of 72 examples were generated, expressed as {N', W, D}, and included parameters in three dimensions (number of patients, number of home care workers, and planning period). These examples contained 24 large-scale examples, 24 medium-scale examples, and 24 small-scale examples; the category parameters are provided in Table 5.8.

2. Performance Metrics

The two heuristic algorithms described above are able to obtain the approximate Pareto front. Therefore, it is necessary to determine the evaluation metrics so that the performance of the algorithms can be analysed through a comparison with the Pareto front. The evaluation focuses on the distance to the Pareto front and the diversity of the solutions. Three evaluation metrics widely used in existing literature are adopted in this study.

The first is the distance metric from the reference set, I_D, which represents the distance between the approximate and exact Pareto fronts [18]. The smaller the value of I_D, the better is the performance of the algorithm in this respect. Given the approximate non-dominated solution set A and the reference solution set R, I_D is calculated as follows:

$$I_D(A, R) = \frac{1}{|R|} \sum_{y \in R} \min_{x \in A} d(x, y) \tag{5.25}$$

in which, $d(x, y)$ is the distance between solution x (belonging to set A) and solution y (belonging to set R), which is calculated as follows:

$$d(x, y) = \sqrt{\sum_{i=1}^{M} \left(\frac{f_i(x) - f_i(y)}{f_i^{max} - f_i^{min}} \right)^2} \tag{5.26}$$

In Eq. (5.26), M is the number of objectives; and f_i^{min} and f_i^{max} ($i \in [1, M]$) are the maximum and minimum values, respectively, of the ith objective function in set R.

Theoretically, the reference set R in the metric expression refers to the exact Pareto front. However, the exact solution set is often difficult to obtain, especially for large-scale problems. Therefore, the union set of the solution sets obtained by the two algorithms is used as the reference set R.

The second is the set coverage metric $C(A, B)$. Given two non-dominated solution sets A and B, this metric is used to calculate the dominance relationship between the two solution sets [19]. This metric is calculated as follows:

$$C(A, B) = \frac{|\{x \in B | \exists y \in A : y \geq x\}|}{|B|} \tag{5.27}$$

in which, $y \geq x$ indicates that solution y is non-dominated relative to solution x. $C(A, B) \in [0, 1]$, $C(A, B) = 0$ indicates that for any solution in set A, a non-dominated solution can always be found in set B; $C(A, B) = 1$ indicates the opposite. Both $C(A, B)$ and $C(B, A)$ between sets A and B need to be calculated; if $C(A, B) > C(B, A)$, the coverage of set A is higher than that of set B.

The third is the maximum span metric MS, which is used to illustrate the coverage span of the non-dominated solution set [20]. This metric is calculated by Eq. (5.28) using set R mentioned in the first metric as the reference set; the larger the value of MS, the wider is the coverage of the objective function value of set A.

$$MS(A) = \sqrt{\sum_{i=1}^{M} \left(\max_{x \in A} \frac{f_i(x) - f_i^{min}}{f_i^{max} - f_i^{min}} - \min_{x \in A} \frac{f_i(x) - f_i^{min}}{f_i^{max} - f_i^{min}} \right)^2} \tag{5.28}$$

3. Parameter tests

The performance of NSGA-II is affected by parameter settings in the algorithm, i.e., population size, number of generations, crossover probability, and mutation probability. Therefore, to select appropriate parameters, parameter tests were conducted before the numerical experiment. A total of 16 parameter combinations were formed based on the above four parameters. Specifically, the following parameter values were used: (1) population size, pop = {100,500}, representing small-scale and large-scale populations, respectively; (2) number of generations, gen = {20, 50}, representing different stages of evolution; and (3) crossover probability, p_c = {0.9,0.7} and mutation probability p_m = {0.1,0.3}, based on the parameters commonly used in genetic algorithms [21].

Small-scale numerical examples were used in parameter tests, and their exact Pareto fronts could be obtained through the ε-constraint algorithm, making the calculation of performance metrics in the parameter tests more accurate. Each example was tested 10 times independently to reduce random errors in the results. The calculation results are provided in Table 5.9, in which the value of I_D is the average of the results from the 10 tests. Based on the evaluation criterion for this metric, the parameter combination corresponding to the minimum value of I_D (indicated by the boldfaced number in the table) was selected. Therefore, in the

Table 5.9 Calculation results for NSGA-II parameter tests

{pop,gen,pc,pm}	I_D	{pop,gen,pc,pm}	I_D
{100,20,0.9,0.1}	0.414	{500,20,0.9,0.1}	0.365
{100,20,0.9,0.3}	0.393	{500,20,0.9,0.3}	0.368
{100,20,0.7,0.1}	0.401	{500,20,0.7,0.1}	0.371
{100,20,0.7,0.3}	0.387	{500,20,0.7,0.3}	0.377
{100,50,0.9,0.1}	0.369	{500,50,0.9,0.1}	**0.307**
{100,50,0.9,0.3}	0.344	{500,50,0.9,0.3}	0.320
{100,50,0.7,0.1}	0.362	{500,50,0.7,0.1}	0.316
{100,50,0.7,0.3}	0.350	{500,50,0.7,0.3}	0.322

subsequent numerical experiments, the parameters of NSGA-II were set as pop = 500, gen = 50, p_c = 0.9, and p_m = 0.1.

4. Results and Analysis

In the numerical experiment, both NSGA-II and the random assignment algorithm were applied to 72 examples; the ε-constraint algorithm was only applied to 24 small-scale examples due to its relatively long computation time. For each example, 10 independent tests were performed, and the values for each of the three metrics from the 10 tests were calculated and averaged. In addition, the computation time for each algorithm was also recorded in the table as the fourth metric.

For small-scale numerical examples, the exact Pareto fronts were obtained by the ε-constraint algorithm and used as the reference set for calculating the metrics of the heuristic algorithms. The values for the four metrics from 10 tests of the 24 small-scale numerical examples are provided in Table 5.10. The average computation time of the 10 runs of the ε-constraint algorithm is shown in the last column of the table. Due to its long computation time, the ε-constraint algorithm failed to obtain all the 10 test results for three small-scale examples (i.e., {7, 3, 7}, {8, 2, 7}, and {8, 4, 7}) within 3 h; specifically, for each of these three examples, results were obtained for 9 out of 10 tests, and an error message of 'out of memory' was reported for the tenth test. For this reason, the computation time for each of these three numerical examples was averaged using the nine successful numerical runs.

The computation time for the ε-constraint algorithm was significantly longer than that for the other two algorithms and was not stable, the shortest being 22 s and the longest being over 1000 s. The computation time for NSGA-II was approximately 80 s, while that for the random assignment algorithm was extremely short, consistently less than 1 s. The ε-constraint algorithm can be used as a benchmark in calculating I_D, $C(A, B)$, and MS values, NSGA-II and the random assignment algorithm both have a $C(A, B)$ value of 0; therefore, the obtained approximate solutions cannot be superior to the exact solutions. Compared with NSGA-II, the random assignment algorithm has a small I_D value but a large MS value, albeit with only slight differences, indicating that the random assignment algorithm slightly outperforms NSGA-II in solving small-scale problems.

Table 5.10 Comparison of the results for small-scale numerical examples

Example	NSGA-II (denoted as A)				Random assignment algorithm (denoted as B)				ε-constraint (denoted as C)
	I_D	$C(A, C)$	MS	Time	I_D	$C(B, C)$	MS	Time	Time
{5, 2, 5}	0.161	0	0.674	68.847	0.208	0	0.733	0.052	22.800
{5, 2, 7}	0.267	0	0.486	70.826	0.056	0	0.618	0.055	38.697
{5, 3, 5}	0.247	0	0.532	71.553	0.061	0	0.596	0.059	44.035
{5, 3, 7}	0.283	0	0.482	74.473	0.046	0	0.487	0.068	67.100
{5, 4, 5}	0.235	0	0.557	74.327	0.053	0	0.590	0.063	69.074
{5, 4, 7}	0.282	0	0.475	78.170	0.041	0	0.540	0.078	103.795
{6, 2, 5}	0.174	0	0.664	70.780	0.064	0	0.703	0.060	51.779
{6, 2, 7}	0.235	0	0.540	73.662	0.043	0	0.603	0.073	73.241
{6, 3, 5}	0.220	0	0.548	74.661	0.041	0	0.619	0.074	86.641
{6, 3, 7}	0.251	0	0.501	78.895	0.124	0	0.631	0.097	133.278
{6, 4, 5}	0.215	0	0.557	77.761	0.189	0	0.702	0.097	127.948
{6, 4, 7}	0.281	0	0.469	82.496	0.104	0	0.514	0.098	298.011
{7, 2, 5}	0.171	0	0.634	73.329	0.116	0	0.850	0.079	95.842
{7, 2, 7}	0.230	0	0.533	77.071	0.019	0	0.632	0.088	138.564
{7, 3, 5}	0.264	0	0.487	76.961	0.315	0	0.482	0.084	173.447
{7, 3, 7}	0.327	0	0.375	81.713	0.369	0	0.404	0.119	291.509
{7, 4, 5}	0.241	0	0.512	81.693	0.236	0	0.577	0.108	191.098
{7, 4, 7}	0.297	0	0.375	86.176	0.059	0	0.464	0.144	1882.768
{8, 2, 5}	0.186	0	0.546	75.309	0.159	0	0.648	0.089	104.274
{8, 2, 7}	0.245	0	0.488	79.444	0.230	0	0.554	0.115	126.549
{8, 3, 5}	0.268	0	0.434	79.801	0.209	0	0.559	0.127	164.292
{8, 3, 7}	0.311	0	0.383	85.186	0.219	0	0.484	0.154	246.777
{8, 4, 5}	0.271	0	0.455	84.805	0.284	0	0.517	0.146	427.556
{8, 4, 7}	0.356	0	0.343	89.279	0.306	0	0.377	0.145	1122.143
Average	0.251	0	0.502	77.801	**0.148**	0	**0.578**	**0.095**	253.384

For medium-scale numerical examples, the ε-constraint algorithm was unable to obtain accurate solutions within a reasonable time. Therefore, only the performances of NSGA-II and the random assignment algorithm were compared. The values for the metrics of the two algorithms for the 24 medium-scale examples are provided in Table 5.11; each reported result is the average of those from 10 independent runs. The I_D values for both algorithms are small (less than 0.1), but overall, the random assignment algorithm outperformed NSGA-II, indicating that the Pareto front obtained by the random assignment algorithm is closer to the exact solutions. The average $C(A, B)$ value for the NSGA-II algorithm is larger than that for the random assignment algorithm, indicating that NSGA-II resulted in more non-dominated solutions. In terms of the MS metric, the solutions obtained by the random assignment algorithm were more widely distributed. In summary, the above analyses

Table 5.11 Comparison of the results for medium-scale numerical examples

Example	NSGA-II (denoted as A)				Random assignment algorithm (denoted as B)			
	I_D	$C(A,B)$	MS	Time	I_D	$C(B,A)$	MS	Time
{25, 8, 5}	0.080	0.706	0.928	198.525	0.033	0	1.394	3.345
{25, 8, 7}	0.074	0.738	0.945	260.728	0.033	0	1.391	4.557
{25, 10, 5}	0.077	0.744	0.943	234.217	0.037	0	1.381	4.190
{25, 10, 7}	0.067	0.738	0.980	325.862	0.037	0.003	1.367	5.754
{25, 12, 5}	0.090	0.738	0.903	276.366	0.040	0	1.405	5.019
{25, 12, 7}	0.073	0.764	0.977	400.618	0.043	0	1.405	6.881
{30, 8, 5}	0.096	0.601	0.773	233.264	0.027	0.008	1.409	5.892
{30, 8, 7}	0.074	0.706	0.927	319.055	0.028	0	1.402	7.510
{30, 10, 5}	0.075	0.672	0.936	284.113	0.032	0.02	1.382	6.988
{30, 10, 7}	0.075	0.769	0.970	405.784	0.039	0	1.407	9.271
{30, 12, 5}	0.084	0.669	0.973	340.598	0.033	0.04	1.385	8.173
{30, 12, 7}	0.075	0.778	0.992	498.239	0.041	0	1.381	11.047
{35, 8, 5}	0.076	0.551	0.867	276.560	0.019	0.041	1.381	8.538
{35, 8, 7}	0.080	0.613	0.915	385.965	0.024	0.037	1.385	12.117
{35, 10, 5}	0.086	0.551	0.838	341.763	0.021	0.043	1.392	10.909
{35, 10, 7}	0.082	0.659	0.830	497.752	0.029	0	1.414	14.966
{35, 12, 5}	0.088	0.641	0.879	411.700	0.029	0.021	1.397	13.002
{35, 12, 7}	0.088	0.698	0.904	605.535	0.039	0.012	1.396	17.332
{40, 8, 5}	0.103	0.329	0.843	328.184	0.016	0.345	1.374	12.952
{40, 8, 7}	0.087	0.560	0.863	463.424	0.019	0.036	1.393	17.447
{40, 10, 5}	0.096	0.174	0.883	426.428	0.012	0.696	1.384	15.989
{40, 10, 7}	0.080	0.614	0.910	599.151	0.027	0.038	1.361	21.315
{40, 12, 5}	0.093	0.295	0.898	496.980	0.015	0.401	1.359	18.676
{40, 12, 7}	0.080	0.686	0.929	733.637	0.031	0.013	1.391	26.025
Average	0.083	**0.625**	0.908	389.352	**0.029**	0.073	**1.389**	**11.162**

indicate that the random assignment algorithm performs better in solving medium-scale problems.

For large-scale numerical examples, the four metrics of the two heuristic algorithms were similarly compared, with the results provided in Table 5.12. Overall, the random assignment algorithm outperformed NSGA-II, i.e., when solving large-scale problems, the random assignment algorithm can obtain a better Pareto front within a shorter time.

To visually illustrate the performance of the two heuristic algorithms, the Pareto curves obtained from the medium-scale and large-scale examples are plotted in a coordinate system, as shown in Figs. 5.4 and 5.5, respectively. '+' and '*' curves represent the NSGA-II and random assignment algorithm results, respectively, and the x- and y-axes represent the values for objective function 1 (i.e., operating cost) and objective function 2 (i.e., patient satisfaction, which was multiplied by -1 to minimise the objective function for simplified computation). Figure 5.4 shows the results for medium-scale numerical examples; a larger number of non-dominated solutions were obtained by NSGA-II, with more widely distributed non-dominated

Table 5.12 Comparison of the results for large-scale numerical examples

Example	NSGA-II (denoted as A)				Random assignment algorithm (denoted as B)			
	I_D	$C(A,B)$	MS	Time	I_D	$C(B,A)$	MS	Time
{50,14,5}	0.123	0.166	0.823	809.407	0.026	0.704	1.354	44.382
{50,14,7}	0.100	0.419	0.873	1098.419	0.020	0.270	1.369	63.756
{50,16,5}	0.126	0.223	0.845	952.559	0.020	0.557	1.398	58.940
{50,16,7}	0.115	0.301	0.836	1304.242	0.016	0.444	1.374	79.793
{50,18,5}	0.165	0.015	0.733	1033.825	0.021	0.971	1.384	59.935
{50,18,7}	0.119	0.459	0.868	1455.145	0.029	0.254	1.408	78.523
{55,14,5}	0.152	0.002	0.803	912.176	0.042	0.998	1.351	60.123
{55,14,7}	0.102	0.371	0.900	1268.411	0.024	0.366	1.357	80.880
{55,16,5}	0.169	0	0.799	1073.530	0.038	1.000	1.389	77.627
{55,16,7}	0.110	0.380	0.827	1463.716	0.017	0.280	1.370	104.904
{55,18,5}	0.168	0	0.786	1179.806	0.029	1.000	1.366	75.830
{55,18,7}	0.115	0.371	0.786	1638.161	0.016	0.264	1.395	105.182
{60,14,5}	0.195	0	0.757	1039.575	0.035	1.000	1.369	77.382
{60,14,7}	0.134	0.166	0.830	1429.595	0.024	0.264	1.358	109.329
{60,16,5}	0.196	0	0.758	1197.821	0.031	1.000	1.344	95.487
{60,16,7}	0.128	0.214	0.835	1684.372	0.019	0.636	1.368	145.178
{60,18,5}	0.177	0	0.791	1341.470	0.069	1.000	1.336	99.045
{60,18,7}	0.126	0.252	0.838	1868.057	0.030	0.447	1.388	153.355
{65,14,5}	0.198	0	0.753	1169.780	0.079	1.000	1.335	103.910
{65,14,7}	0.149	0.033	0.780	1607.733	0.037	0.932	1.346	154.583
{65,16,5}	0.214	0	0.745	1358.927	0.037	1.000	1.319	122.213
{65,16,7}	0.158	0.044	0.786	1875.988	0.026	0.919	1.404	184.599
{65,18,5}	0.219	0	0.716	1539.293	0.036	1.000	1.386	135.663
{65,18,7}	0.135	0.094	0.845	2125.078	0.046	0.819	1.342	198.504
Average	0.150	0.146	0.805	1351.129	**0.032**	**0.731**	**1.367**	**102.880**

solutions by the random assignment algorithm. Figure 5.5 shows the results for the large-scale numerical examples; the random assignment algorithm is superior to NSGA-II. The results are consistent with the data provided in the tables.

The results of the numerical experiments also indicate that both NSGA-II and the random assignment algorithm can effectively solve the home care worker scheduling problem. In particular, the random assignment algorithm is superior for solving large-scale problems, and NSGA-II is more suitable for solving medium-scale problems. For small-scale problems, the two algorithms are comparable in terms of solution effectiveness. For medium-scale problems, the solution set obtained by the random assignment algorithm is closer to the reference set and more widely distributed, and NSGA-II can obtain a larger number of non-dominated solutions. For large-scale problems, the random assignment algorithm significantly outperforms NSGA-II. In summary, when solving the actual home care worker scheduling problem, the random assignment algorithm should be used for large-scale problems, and NSGA-II should be used for medium-scale problems.

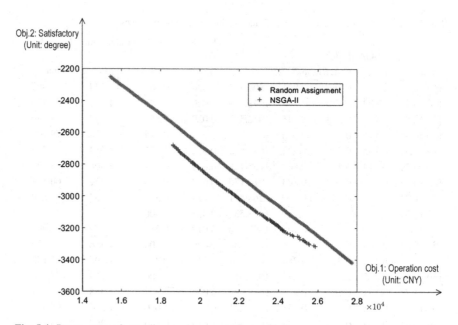

Fig. 5.4 Pareto curves for medium-scale numerical examples

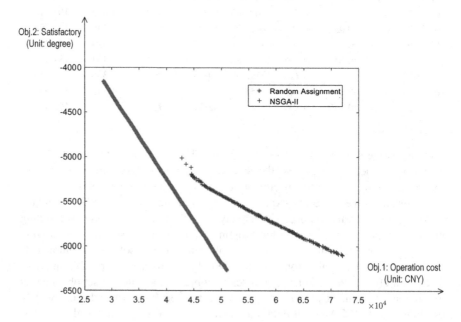

Fig. 5.5 Pareto curves for large-scale numerical examples

References

1. M. Stuart, M. Weinrich, Home-and community-based long-term care. Lessons from Denmark. Gerontologist **41**(4), 474–480 (2001)
2. F. Wang, Z. Lu, Main features of the UK health service delivery model and health care system. For. Med. Sci. **22**(4), 145–149 (2005)
3. Y. Zhang, Comparisons of community health service models at home and abroad. Chin. Health Serv. Manag. **7**, 419–420 (2003)
4. C. Seott, *Public and Private Roles in Health Care Systems: Reform Experience in Seven OECD Countries* (UK Open University Press, Buckingham, 2001), pp. 73–74
5. M.S.R. Wagstaff, *A System Wide Impacts of Hospital Payment Reforms: Evidence from Central and Eastern Europe and Central Asia* (The World Bank Development Research Group, Human Development and Public Services Team, 2009)
6. Q. Li, Community health service in Germany and Sweden. Clin. Educ. of Gen. Pract. **3**(4), 196–200 (2005)
7. L. Liu, C. Lu, The delivery system of community health services in Australia and insights. Chin. Gen. Pract. **5**(1), 40–42 (2002)
8. C. Grant, H.M. Lapeley, *The Australian Health Care System* (Marrickville Southward Press, 1993), pp. 61–90
9. C. Jiang, Characteristics and enlightenment of community services in Hong Kong. Tan Qiu (Exploration) **139**(76), 70–73
10. S. Hu, *Comparative Study of Medical Insurance Payment Methods* (Shanghai Science and Technology Press, 2010)
11. X. Wang, Payment mechanism in medical insurance system. Chin. Hosp. Manag. **19**(4), 10–12 (1999)
12. W. Liang, General medicine, general practice, and general practitioners. Chin. J. Sch. Health (2004)
13. C. Vira, Y.Y. Haimes, *Multi-Objective Decision Making: Theory and Methodology* (North-Holland, 1983)
14. K. Miettinen, *Nonlinear Multi-Objective Optimization*, International Series in Operations Research and Management Science, vol 12 (1999)
15. J.F. Bérubé, M. Gendreau, J.Y. Potvin, An exact ε-constraint method for bi-objective combinatorial optimization problems: application to the traveling salesman problem with Pro_ts. Eur. J. Oper. Res. **194**(1), 39–50 (2009)
16. K. Deb, A. Pratap, S. Agarwal, T. Meyarivan, A fast and elitist multi-objective genetic algorithm: NSGA-II. IEEE Trans. Evol. Comput. **6**(2), 182–197 (2002)
17. D.S. Johnson, L.A. McGeoch, The traveling salesman problem: a case study in local optimization. Loc. Sear. Combinat. Optimiz. **1**, 215–310 (1997)
18. C.A.C. Coello, N.C. Cortes, Solving multiobjective optimization problems using an artificial immune system. Genet. Program Evolvable Mach. **6**(2), 163–190 (2005)
19. E. Zitzler, L. Thiele, M. Laumanns, C.M. Fonseca, V.G. da Fonseca, Performance assessment of multi-objective optimizers: an analysis and review. IEEE Trans. Evol. Comput. **7**(2), 117–132 (2003)
20. E. Zitzler, K. Deb, L. Thiele, Comparison of multi-objective evolutionary algorithms: empirical results. Evol. Comput. **8**(2), 173–195 (2000)
21. C. Oguz, M.F. Ercan, A genetic algorithm for hybrid flow shop scheduling with multiprocessor tasks. J. Sched. **8**(4), 323–335 (2005)

Printed in the United States
by Baker & Taylor Publisher Services